LIFE NATURE LIBRARY

THE LAND AND WILDLIFE OF
AUSTRALIA

OTHER BOOKS
BY THE EDITORS OF LIFE

LIFE WORLD LIBRARY
LIFE SCIENCE LIBRARY
THE LIFE HISTORY OF THE UNITED STATES
LIFE PICTORIAL ATLAS OF THE WORLD
THE EPIC OF MAN
THE WONDERS OF LIFE ON EARTH
THE WORLD WE LIVE IN
THE WORLD'S GREAT RELIGIONS
THE LIFE BOOK OF CHRISTMAS
LIFE'S PICTURE HISTORY OF WESTERN MAN
THE LIFE TREASURY OF AMERICAN FOLKLORE
AMERICA'S ARTS AND SKILLS
THE SECOND WORLD WAR
LIFE'S PICTURE HISTORY OF WORLD WAR II
PICTURE COOK BOOK
LIFE GUIDE TO PARIS

LIFE NATURE LIBRARY

THE LAND AND WILDLIFE OF
AUSTRALIA

by David Bergamini
and The Editors of LIFE

TIME INCORPORATED
NEW YORK

A
STONEHENGE
BOOK

About the Author

Monotremes, marsupials, foxes that fly and birds that don't are familiar creatures to David Bergamini, who has experienced the oddities of nature's extremes on journeys from Southeast Asia to the rain forests of Brazil. A member of the staff that produced *The World We Live In*, and later a free-lance writer and picture researcher, he spent 10 years gaining valuable insight and experience in the problem of writing about the flora and fauna of remote areas, where the evidence is fragmentary and the opinions of experts often contradictory. Earlier books by Mr. Bergamini are *The Universe*, written for the LIFE Nature Library; *Mathematics*, written for the LIFE Science Library; and *The Fleet in the Window*, a novel based on his experiences in a Japanese prison camp in the Philippines during World War II. Married, he lives with his wife and four children in Rowayton, Connecticut.

ON THE COVER: A koala mother and baby wake from their all-day sleep in an Australian sanctuary. Koalas must have a variety of fresh *Eucalyptus* leaves for food every day, and as a result they are almost never seen alive outside of Australia.

Contents

TIME / LIFE BOOKS

Editor: NORMAN P. ROSS
Text Director: WILLIAM JAY GOLD   *Art Director:* EDWARD A. HAMILTON
Chief of Research: BEATRICE T. DOBIE

EDITORIAL STAFF FOR "THE LAND AND WILDLIFE OF AUSTRALIA"

Editor, LIFE Nature Library: MAITLAND A. EDEY
Assistant to the Editor: ROBERT MORTON
Copy Editor: PERCY KNAUTH
Designer: PAUL JENSEN
Staff Writers: DALE BROWN, DORIS BRY, MARY LOUISE GROSSMAN, PETER WOOD
Chief Researcher: MARTHA TURNER
Researchers: GERALD A. BAIR, DAVID BRIDGE, PEGGY BUSHONG, JOHN VON HARTZ,
NAOMI KATZ, LECLAIR G. LAMBERT, CAROL PHILLIPPE, NANCY SHUKER, IRIS UNGER
Picture Researchers: MARGARET K. GOLDSMITH, JOAN LYNCH
Art Associate: ROBERT L. YOUNG
Art Assistants: JAMES D. SMITH, MARK A. BINN, JOHN NEWCOMB
Copy Staff: MARIAN GORDON GOLDMAN, JOAN CHAMBERS, DOLORES A. LITTLES

Publisher: JEROME S. HARDY
General Manager: JOHN A. WATTERS

LIFE MAGAZINE

Editor   *Managing Editor*   *Publisher*
EDWARD K. THOMPSON   GEORGE P. HUNT   C. D. JACKSON

The text for the chapters of this book was written by David Bergamini, the picture essays
by the editorial staff. The following individuals and departments of Time Inc. were helpful
in producing the book: John Dominis, Fritz Goro, Ralph Morse, George Silk, LIFE staff photographers; Doris O'Neil, Chief of the LIFE Picture Library; Philip W. Payne of the TIME-
LIFE News Service; and Content Peckham, Chief of the Time Inc. Bureau of Editorial Reference.

Introduction

To many biologists, Australasia—the Australian continent with its outlying islands—is the most interesting region in the world. Its flora and fauna are a bizarre mixture of the primitive and the advanced, and provide better glimpses into some of the basic processes of evolution than those of any other continental area. The insular nature of the whole region—the continent itself has been isolated for at least 60 million years—makes it possible for scientists to observe how one particular group, in this case the marsupials, has been allowed to radiate with a minimum of interference by outside influences; and how at the same time a continental fauna may be built up on an original population by a series of invasions and superimpositions, as in the case of Australia's birds.

Because they impose something like laboratory conditions on a natural environment, islands have always been fascinating to evolutionists, from the time of Darwin and Wallace to the present day. Islands not only allow primitive types to survive, but they also have other, equally interesting effects. How do creatures get to them across the water? Some fly—New Zealand has only two types of mammals, but both are bats which clearly arrived on the wing. Others "island hop"—and the Pacific islands in particular show just what groups have this ability and how they go about it. And what happens after a species reaches an island? What it finds may well be an unbalanced nature—i.e., opportunities for life which have gone unexploited simply because other animals had not succeeded in reaching the islands to exploit them. So the new arrivals proceed to fill these vacant niches by diversifying in some cases into ways of life which elsewhere they do not follow at all: that is how New Zealand's birds filled many mammal niches. Sometimes, in the absence of predators and competition, even original abilities are lost, as shown by Australasia's flightless birds—the kiwi, kakapo parrot and woodhen—which adapted completely to life on the ground.

All in all, the Australasian region has been spared many of the violent ups and downs, invasions, superimpositions, blendings and extinctions which have so markedly affected the flora and fauna of the world's other great zoogeographical realms—and yet for all its small size it has a diversity of plants and animals rivaling any of them. What these are, how their evolution is understood today and their significant place in the broad picture of life on earth—all this is set down in an absorbing text by David Bergamini, a writer-journalist with a rare ability for developing the most fascinating aspects of his subject. The Editors of LIFE have illuminated the book with many striking illustrations, including the first pictorial rendering of *Thylacoleo*, the cave lion long known only as a fossil skull. As the second volume in a series devoted to the major natural regions of the world and their wildlife, this is indeed a valuable book.

ALLEN KEAST
Department of Biology
Queen's University, Kingston, Ontario

UNMISTAKABLY AUSTRALIAN, a koala and a great red kangaroo reflect in their strangeness millions of years of evolution on an island continent—itself as unusual as the animals it has helped shape.

1

The Dry Continent

When naturalists divide up the globe according to the realistic nonpolitics of plant and animal geography, they recognize Australia, Tasmania and New Guinea, plus the islands east to the Fijis and south to New Zealand, as a single zone of life which they call Notogaea or simply Australasia. Compared to the other great zoogeographic regions—Eurasia, Africa, Southeast Asia and the two Americas—the Australasian zone is small and in large part arid and inhospitable. But this flat, drought-plagued land supports a magnificently rich and strange collection of wildlife.

Isolated as it is by seas and oceans which surround its various parts, Australasia has developed as a world unto itself. Within its wave-washed frontiers, many of its principal groups of plants and animals have evolved on their own, independent of trends in the world at large. Others have found sanctuary in which to vegetate and survive as relict types similar to forms which elsewhere on earth vanished millions of years ago. The unique tuatara of New Zealand, for instance, persists as the sole survivor of a reptilian line anteceding the lizards and even the dinosaurs. It may have sequestered itself on the rocky coasts of New Zealand as long ago as the Triassic period, roughly 200 million years ago.

Neoceratodus, a venerable one-lunged cousin of the air-breathing fishes that first colonized dry land, may have retired to the seclusion of northeastern Australian rivers even earlier, as much as 350 million years ago.

All told, the Australasian region supports approximately 100,000 species of plants and animals—more in proportion to its size than either Eurasia or North America. No others are as ancient as the tuatara or lungfish, but many are just as bizarre, and most of them are exciting to naturalists because they are "endemics"—forms different from those found anywhere else. In fact, it is fair to say that no other region except perhaps South America has such an intensely individual wildlife.

Part of the reason for this, as we shall see, lies in the very nature of Australasia. The continent and its outlying islands, indeed, make up an area quite unlike any other on earth. Here is no broad range of climatic variations such as is characteristic, say, of Eurasia or the Americas, with temperate and tropical, wet and dry regions. New Zealand has snowy peaks and New Guinea cloud forests, but these are exceptions. Australia the continent, the biggest single part of the Australasian realm, is the dramatic example of a succession of variations on a single theme: aridity. It is relatively the most arid of all the continents.

Roughly 2,500 miles wide from west to east, the whole of Australia can be traversed in half a day by modern jet plane. Such a journey, following the line of 25° south latitude—about on a level with São Paulo—would divide the continent almost exactly in half. Looking alternately out of the left and right side window as one flies, the traveler sees, to the north and to the south, the principal physical features that characterize this extraordinary land and that have shaped its wildlife through its long and isolated history.

The west coast of Australia crosses our flight path at right angles. It extends in a narrow ribbon of lowland some 700 miles to the south on our right and 200 miles to the north on our left. Farther north it slants off at an angle ahead of us toward Arnhem Land and ultimately toward New Guinea, 2,200 miles away across the Arafura Sea in the northeast. A little way up that sloping coast, the Great Sandy Desert sweeps out of the interior until it blends its dunes and scattered tussocks of grass and scrub with the ocean strands along the Eighty-Mile Beach. Looking out the right-hand window, toward the city of Perth, the southwest corner of the continent appears contrastingly lush—wooded, in part, with *Eucalyptus* trees almost as tall as the California redwoods.

A HUNDRED miles of coastal lowlands are crossed in a matter of minutes as we fly east, and then the sparsely vegetated terrain below rises about 1,000 feet to a tableland which stretches ahead of us nearly halfway across Australia. Geologically, this area is incredibly old. The southern section of it has been high and dry for so long that three quarters of its existence had already passed before the first land plants appeared.

Inland from the coast, cattle and sheep ranches, or "stations" as Australians call them, become progressively fewer and farther between. Finally, there are no habitations at all and the only human beings below are tiny bands of nomadic aborigines. To the north sprawls an immense expanse of steppe overgrown with tussocks of *Triodia* grass and patches of dry shrubs. To the south the grass extends in corridors and pockets into a region of what Australians call "mulga," a spindly, saplinglike scrub dominated by one of the 600-odd native acacias. Mulga often grows with dense shrubs that the early travelers sometimes found impenetrable and called "wait-awhile" or "dead-finish."

Farther south still, the mulga gives way to a taller and more open kind of scrub—also typically Australian—called "mallee." This is formed by dwarf eucalypts which grow with multiple stems and hump up, 10 or 20 feet high, out of the surrounding porcupine grass and shrubbery. Still farther south, taller species of eucalypts appear. Mallee gives place to open grassy woodland and this in turn to the magnificent stands of timber in the southwest garden corner of the continent.

Four hundred miles from the coast, the last headwaters of the western rivers have been left behind. There is no true watershed and no new network of rivers on the other side. For the next 900 miles, the plateau will go on and on without any sign of surface drainage except an occasional dry creek bed, an occasional glint of water in a reservoir of natural rock or an occasional salt flat euphemistically labeled "lake" on the map. The elevation of the land varies between 500 and 1,000 feet above sea level, but so gently that from above it appears absolutely flat.

THOUGH featureless and arid, this land is not all desert. It supports a thin cover of grass or mulga, and most of it is watered, if somewhat erratically, by more than the critical 10 inches of rain per year which is normally taken as the upper limit for true desert. About 600 miles from the coast, however, we reach a north-to-south belt of land where the grass grows sparsely and banked sand dunes frequently show themselves. The rainfall still hovers close to the 10-inches-a-year mark, but it comes unpredictably and sometimes all at once so that the vegetation must be capable of withstanding long periods of extreme drought. One locality may drink up its entire annual quota of rain in a couple of afternoons; another that statistically averages eight inches of rain a year may actually enjoy seven or eight swimmingly wet days in a decade.

The portion of this desert belt which now lies directly below our flight path is known as Gibson's Desert. To the northwest, it runs into the Great Sandy Desert. To the southeast, it extends over a range of hills into the Great Victorian Desert. This in turn shelves off into the southern ocean across the Nullarbor Plain, a tremendous sheet of limestone that appears as flat as a concrete roof. Derived from two Latin words, "nul" and "arbor," meaning "no tree," this name appropriately reflects the plain's almost complete want of vegetation except a threadbare cover of saltbush and other small shrubs. The Nullarbor Plain owes its desolation to the fact that its underlying rock is a soft limestone for down to 900 feet. Any water falling on the surface immediately sinks into the limestone and is lost to the plants. Water action has riddled the plain with holes and caverns. Where it abuts on the ocean, it has been carved into breathtaking cliffs—cliffs which run for 120 miles along that huge, shallow southern bay known as the Great Australian Bight. Though not as sterile as the Sahara, the Australian arid belt, arcing northwest from the Bight to the Indian Ocean, interposes a formidable barrier between the southwest and the rest of the continent. Vast tracts are naked of all but a few tufts of grass. These are the gibber or stony desert areas, coated as far as the eye can reach with a shimmering pavement of pebbles.

Beyond the deserts, at almost the dead center of the continent, we reach the fiery red-rock mountains of the Macdonnell and Musgrave ranges. These are outposts of the ancient shield of continental granite which we have already crossed to the west. They rise 2,000 to 4,000 feet above sea level. Over the course of 500 million years they have suffered innumerable vicissitudes and they have

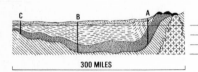

300 MILES

AN UNDERGROUND WATER SUPPLY

This relief map of Australia is drawn in greatly exaggerated vertical scale to accent the continent's principal terrain features: a flat dry western plain, a huge depressed basin to the east of it, and mountains along the eastern coast. The tinted sections show major areas of underground water, on which Australians depend to compensate for the dry climate. The most important of these underlies the Great Basin, getting its supply from rain water which trickles slowly downward and along a stratum of sandstone (colored area in cross section), collecting there in large quantity and under some pressure between impermeable shale above and bedrock beneath it. For wells drilled at certain points, such as C, there is enough pressure to cause water to flow naturally from the ground. But at A or B, it might have to be pumped. The location of this 300-mile cross section is indicated by a broken line on the map.

been worn and broken into fantastic contours. One entire range south of the Macdonnells, mysteriously flat across the top, reveals in its gullies and gorges a spectacular cross section of upwrinkled rock strata.

Between the Macdonnells and Musgraves stand three lonely lumps of obdurate stone which have survived untold ages of weather in peculiar isolation. They sit far apart on an otherwise flat expanse of plain that is splashed with the clear green of kurrajong trees, and the black trunks and graceful drooping foliage of desert oaks, or casuarinas. Ayers Rock is shaped like a gargantuan tortoise shell. Mount Connor is an immense decapitated cone with grassy top and crumbling sides of rubble. The strangest of the three, Mount Olga, consists of rounded monoliths rising precipitously 1,000 to 1,400 feet, clustered so closely that sunlight penetrates the chasms between them for no more than an hour or two each day. So water-retentive is the rock which lines these gorges that the canyon bottoms are overgrown with bushes and low shrubs, vegetation distinctly richer and greener than that of the surrounding sand plains.

THROUGHOUT this central mountain area—the "red center," as it is sometimes called because of the prevailing color of its sand and rocks—the craggy brilliance of the cliffs and the strange vegetation produce a scenery of dramatic loveliness. Except for Alice Springs, a prosperous cattle and mining community, the region is virtually uninhabited, but hardy campers travel for days just for the pleasures of sightseeing. And the thirsty explorers who first discovered it were so struck by its beauties that they nostalgically named its clefts after Celtic glens and gills.

The oasis of central mountain vegetation is entirely surrounded by a high half-desert of mulga. To the south, mulga or outright desert extends all the way to the seacoast. To the north the mulga is succeeded by a grassy steppe and then by a richer grassland known as savanna, which covers the gentle hills of the Barkly Tableland. Farther north, in Arnhem Land, the savannas are studded with groves of eucalypts in a pleasantly mixed plant formation that has the air of a park. This savanna woodland, as it is called, continues to the north coast where it is cut off from the sea by a belt of mangrove swamps.

Having crossed the red center, we come to the end of the great western plateau and the beginning of the central basin. As the land drops away by about a thousand feet, we see the great parallel sand dunes of the Arunta or Simpson desert below. The region south toward Lake Eyre is the driest part of Australia, receiving a pittance of less than five inches of rain a year. Lake Eyre, despite its name, is nothing more than a vast internal drainage sink, a great sub-sea-level salt flat, 150 miles long and 50 miles wide. It is cut off from the south coast by low ridges and mountains. A couple of times within living memory it has been partly covered by a shallow sheet of water and lived up to its name as a lake. But most of the time since European settlement it has lain bone-dry. Many lines labeled "river" on the map converge on Lake Eyre, but they are rivers that run rarely and still more rarely reach their destination.

Eastward from Lake Eyre, the natural vegetation changes little, but, surprisingly, flocks of sheep appear. This is explained by the fact that we are now over the largest artesian basin in the world, more than half a million square miles of subterranean drainage supplied by the runoff from the mountains far to the northeast. When tapped, the underground waters gush up in artesian wells and in some places break through to the surface in peculiar little aqueous volcanoes called "mound springs."

Farther to the east is the one great river system in Australia worthy of the name, the Murray-Darling. This drains the interior of southern Queensland and all of western New South Wales, finally emptying into the sea near the city of Adelaide some 800 miles away.

The Murray-Darling basin is pleasant, flat country and it forms the greatest sheep pasture in the land. Part of it is black soil plain. It is covered in places with *Eucalyptus* woodlands and in others by extensive grasslands or that wonderful sheep fodder, the saltbush. In the drier parts are tracts of mulga or, in the south, of mallee. Every stream bed, big or small, flowing or dry, is lined with majestic, shady river gums. Here and there, after good rains, huge marshes are formed to become the breeding grounds for multitudes of water birds. Rainfall varies from 10 inches annually in the north to more than 20 in the south. But it can fluctuate so capriciously that most of the streams dry away periodically to a chain of pools.

The majestic 1,750-mile Darling, the continent's longest river, has fallen silent for as long as 18 months at a time and is sometimes reduced to a succession of oxbow lakes known as billabongs. Though supposed to empty into the Darling, the waters of the 400-mile Paroo almost never do. Once, in the wet year of 1870, they poured in 60 miles wide, but since then they have normally disappeared to the north, drunk up by their own stream beds.

Beyond the Murray Basin the land gradually rises again to the watershed of the Great Dividing Range. This north-south backbone along the eastern edge of the continent is Australia's principal mountain system. Most Australians live on the narrow, fertile coastal fringe just to the east of it, and many of them still refer to the other 90 per cent of the country to the west as "the outback."

Eastward from the Darling River, mulga gives place to grassland, grassland to savanna forest, and then to thick forests of cypress pine or stands of eucalypts such as we have not seen since leaving the groves near Perth on the other side of the continent. The so-called cypress pines belong to *Callitris*, an endemic Australian conifer genus which is claimed by the botanist R. T. Baker to be the most venerable of all pines in the world and to resemble in the microscopic details of its wood structure a tree which left fossils in Europe some 300 million years ago.

The passes through the mountains beneath us average only about a thousand feet in elevation, but 13 of the peaks are over a mile high, and one massive block to the south tops out in Mount Kosciusko—the continent's highest mountain—with a height of 7,316 feet.

T HE eastern slopes of the mountains, as they plunge toward the Pacific, are considerably steeper than the western approaches. From 30 to over 80 inches of rain pours down on them each year, and they murmur with running waters. Towering *Eucalyptus* forests swarm up the valleys, their tree crowns fitting together loosely and letting in sufficient sunlight for a rich undergrowth. In some of the dampest areas the monopoly of the eucalypts is broken by other associations of trees which classify as rain forests. Of these, there are two opposite kinds: the subantarctic, and the subtropical and tropical forests. The former is found mostly in the south and mostly on the colder ridges of the mountains; the latter lie farther north, leapfrogging down a string of higher rainfall areas from the New Guinea region.

The subantarctic rain forest is dominated by a genus of beech tree, *Nothofagus*, which is common in the cooler sections of the Southern Hemisphere and is

ROCKS OF AUSTRALASIA

Australasia has three distinct types of rocky underpinning. Oldest is the flat, granitic shield that forms the western portion of Australia (shown in pale gray on the map above). It has been stable for more than 600 million years. Eastward the land is somewhat younger and more rugged (dark gray), and was shaped by the mountain building that took place some 100 million years ago. Still farther east lies an unstable, more recently made chain of volcanic islands. They are part of the "ring of fire" (color) that circles the Pacific and accounts for more than 80 per cent of all earthquakes and volcanic eruptions.

believed to have been distinct from the Northern Hemisphere beech, the genus *Fagus*, since at least the end of the Cretaceous. In Australia the stronghold of the southern beech is the craggy western half of Tasmania, where it presides over a subantarctic rain forest that is almost impenetrable in places. Delicate ferns fill the aisles between the gnarled buttress roots of the dripping trees, and the whole undergrowth is woven together by a curious saxifrage called the "horizontal." This maddening plant grows four or five feet high on a stem so weak that it soon falls over and starts afresh. Then new stems shoot upward out of the old, only to fall over in their turn. Ultimately one horizontal may surround itself with a thicket that has all the obstructionary qualities of a field heaped with fishnets and staked out wildly with fence pickets.

In contrast to the subantarctic woodlands of beech, the subtropical rain forest is distinguished by the enormous variety of the trees which compose it and the canopy formed by their interlocking crowns. So little light comes through to ground level that underbrush grows sparsely. Except around holes and breaks rent by the fall of a tree, or where dense lawyer vines tear at clothes and face, walking is easy and the walker can enjoy the peculiar rain forest sights: the aboveground roots which buttress the trees, the contortions of lianas and strangler figs, the glimpses of overhead orchids.

RAIN forest and *Eucalyptus* forest; savanna woodland and savanna; mulga and mallee; steppe and gibber plain; basin, plateau and mountain range —what do they all signify in the evolutionary history of Australia? According to the principles enunciated by modern evolutionists, stocks of plants and animals branch out into separate species and genera because their offspring become isolated from one another and evolve separately until they become so differentiated that they are no longer capable of interbreeding. The reason they become isolated is that they spread into different regions and can no longer mingle. The reason they evolve is that each land and life they adopt tends to put a premium on different qualities which may be latent in their genes and may be brought out through natural breeding over many generations. In this process two factors are necessary—some initial variability in the genes of the pioneering creatures so that evolution will have something to work with, and a variety of niches in the environment for them to adjust to through specialization.

Considering the small number of immigrants that are believed to have colonized Australia, and the genetic limitations that this implies, it is probable that the isolations provided by the environment itself must have played a major role in calling forth the present diversity of the wildlife. These isolations are not ordinary ones. In North America, high mountain ranges, wide rivers and extremes of climate isolate populations of creatures and abet them in their diversification. In Australia, however, mountains are not high and rivers are not numerous. Temperature barriers, too, as we have seen, are subdued by the moderating influence of the enveloping ocean: far from having distinct arctic, subarctic, temperate, subtropic and tropic belts, Australasia stretches from the equator immediately north of New Guinea almost halfway to the South Pole in Tasmania without dropping off more than about 35° in mean annual temperature. At any latitude along the way, the seasonal fluctuations are equally slight—rarely as much as 30°. As a result, the plants and animals of Rabaul in New Britain and of Tasmania some 2,500 miles closer to the pole are less separated by adaptation to temperature than the creatures from top to bottom on any respectable Alp—or, for that matter, on any tall mountains in New Guinea.

Nevertheless, temperatures do play a part in Australian wildlife. Queensland in the north is warmer than Victoria in the south. It is closer to New Guinea and more accessible to tropical forms of life filtering down from Malaysia. More significantly, however, it receives the bulk of its rain at a different time of the year from Victoria.

The northern and southern coasts of Australia are subject to two different oceanic weather systems. The north gets most of its rain in the hot summer months of December, January and February from Indian Ocean monsoons. The south, on the other hand, is watered during the cool winter months of June, July and August by circumpolar westerlies off the Antarctic Ocean. Varieties of plants and animals on the south coast, obeying instincts which have evolved in response to their environment, seed or breed mainly in the spring, when the damp luxuriance of winter has assured a good supply of food for young ones. In the north, contrariwise, creatures tend to reproduce in the hot, wet summer. Between the two weather systems, throughout most of the arid interior, stray rain clouds from north or south empty their contents in such a haphazard fashion that the desert creatures generally breed whenever a wet spell affords them the opportunity.

It is tempting to speculate that the different breeding cycles experienced in different parts of the country act as isolating mechanisms which in turn serve the process of evolution. More likely, however, it is that the deserts of Central Australia, by sending out long, dry fingers of arid land toward the coasts, isolate the four corners of the continent climatically, and that it is this kind of isolation that has led to the evolutionary differences that have manifested themselves in the different regions.

The only possible rival of aridity in shaping the present community of Australian life has been insularity. Not only is the mainland itself a big island, but it is surrounded by smaller islands which, during the past, have been periodically dropped and picked up again by the coastline. Such nearby outposts as Tasmania, Kangaroo Island and Flinders Island are all thought to have been connected to the continent during a period of lowered sea level in the last 20,000 years. Some of these have their own distinct varieties of plants and animals ready to contribute to the continental melting pot at the next great land rise or ocean fall.

O F all the islands which have been joined to the mainland in the recent past, by far the largest is New Guinea. It is one of the richest in its plants, its animals and even its mixture of human races. Its tropical warmth and luxuriant rainfall make for a dense population of wildlife. Its rugged terrain affords plenty of isolation for the development of new species on high mountains and in remote valleys. Its majestic summits, towering to more than 16,000 feet, are perennially free of snow up to 14,000 or 15,000 feet and are clad in thick forests up to 10,000 to 12,000 feet.

The plants and animals that enjoy this lush environment appear to come from strikingly different backgrounds. The majority of the vertebrate animals —the mammals, birds, reptiles and amphibians—seem most closely related to Australian forms. The majority of the plants, on the other hand, seem most closely related to Asiatic forms.

Only one of the 600-odd Australian eucalypts has adapted itself to the prevailing plant formation of tropical rain forest. This is *Eucalyptus deglupta*, which is found, here and there, towering above the other trees in areas of immaturely developed rain forest all the way from New Britain to the Philippines. It is thought to seed in areas which have been burned over during a dry spell and to grow so rapidly that it gains dominance over other young trees.

The over-all pattern of Asiatic plants and Australian animals in New Guinea must mean that large numbers of plants have been able to cross the water barriers from the north while large numbers of animals have not. Naturalists generally accept this conclusion but differ radically as to its implications. Some of those who believe in continental drift think that New Guinea has always been an outpost of Asia; that Australia has floated up against it only fairly recently; that the two have since merged their faunas extensively but have kept their floras distinct because of the differences between them in warmth and wetness. The more widely accepted view is that New Guinea has served from time immemorial as an entryway and distribution center for Asiatic newcomers to the Australasian region; that seeds borne by birds, wind and water have arrived far more frequently than animals; that both plants and animals have been mainly rain forest creatures which found in New Guinea an environment similar to what they had left in the East Indies; and that many plants which went on to penetrate Australia proper had to adapt to aridity and were transformed radically and distinctively in the process.

WEST of New Guinea, along the chains of the easternmost Spice Islands to the shores of Java and Borneo, Australasian forms of life become progressively more scarce and Malaysian ones more plentiful. At the western edge of this transition zone, the outermost limits of Australasian life are roughly marked by a famous zoogeographical boundary known as the Wallace Line. Alfred Wallace, who first mapped it, is celebrated for having independently hit upon parts of the theory of evolution and for having thereby forced the cautious Charles Darwin into publishing his own long and carefully considered opus on the subject, *The Origin of Species*.

Wallace discerned a frontier between the Australian and Asiatic regions of life during an eight-year study of the East Indies on which he reported in 1869 in his fascinating classic, *The Malay Archipelago*. As he conceived it, the frontier passed south of the Philippines, turned down between Borneo and Celebes, and then threaded its way between the twin islands of Bali and Lombok off the east end of Java. He was particularly struck by the fact that Bali and Lombok, though less than 20 miles apart, have almost completely different bird populations. Bali, for instance, has Asiatic barbets, fruit thrushes and woodpeckers, whereas Lombok to the east has Australasian cockatoos, honey eaters and mound-building incubator birds. Later students of the two islands have endorsed the distinctions noticed by Wallace. One ornithologist, J. A. Leach, has gone so far as to say that the two islands "differ more from each other in their birds and quadrupeds than do England and Japan."

The observations made by Wallace have held up better than the interpretations he placed on them. He conceived of his line as a more or less hard-and-fast boundary, whereas modern naturalists consider it one edge of an extensive smudge in the zoogeographic picture. A few Australasian birds, lizards and plants, for instance, do extend to the west of it into the Asiatic empire, and many Asiatic creatures have spread far to the east of it. The zone of transition or filtration which it initiates, however, is altogether a real one. It has stood the test, not of 100 years, but of at least 50 million years. In fact it has served as the main isolating mechanism in the shaping of Australian wildlife.

THESE HILLS—THE FLINDERS—ARE CONSIDERED MOUNTAINS IN AUSTRALIA, WHERE ONLY 7 PER CENT OF THE LAND RISES ABOVE 2,000 FEET

The Look of the Land

Almost as big as the United States, Australia is far more arid and flat—and yet it is not without contrasts and grandeur. Rain forests stand close by deserts; lakes and rivers run wet and dry; monolithic rocks crop up where least expected. And in the outlying islands—New Guinea, Tasmania, New Zealand—mountains crowd mountains to produce some of the world's most dramatic scenery.

17

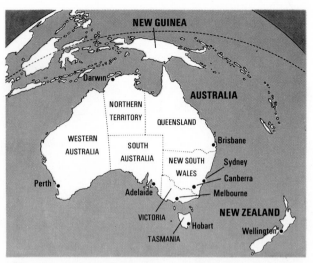

THE AUSTRALASIAN REALM includes, in addition to Australia itself, Tasmania, New Zealand, the islands to the northeast and New Guinea. All have a related flora and fauna.

The Face
of a Continent

Australia, despite the rather wrinkled look of the relief and vegetation map at right, is a phenomenally flat country. It is not so flat, however, that the Highlands along the east coast fail to have a bearing on the kind of weather the continent gets and the kinds of plants that grow there. The Highlands prevent the trade winds that blow in off the Coral and Tasman seas from penetrating into the interior with their gift of rain. And though seasonal rain-bearing storms break over the northern and southern margins of the continent, they soon dissipate themselves. Thus, more than one million square miles receive less than 10 inches of rain a year.

The colored areas on the map show what grows where in Australia, in response to differences in rainfall. Along the east coast, where the annual precipitation ranges from 30 inches to over 100, rain forests and sclerophyll forests, made up of trees with thick-skinned leaves, form the natural ground cover. But farther south and inland—where the rain is infrequent, unreliable or both—the vegetation ranges from mallee scrub (dwarf eucalypts) and mulga scrub (dwarf acacias) to a variety of grasses, all variously adapted to get by on little water.

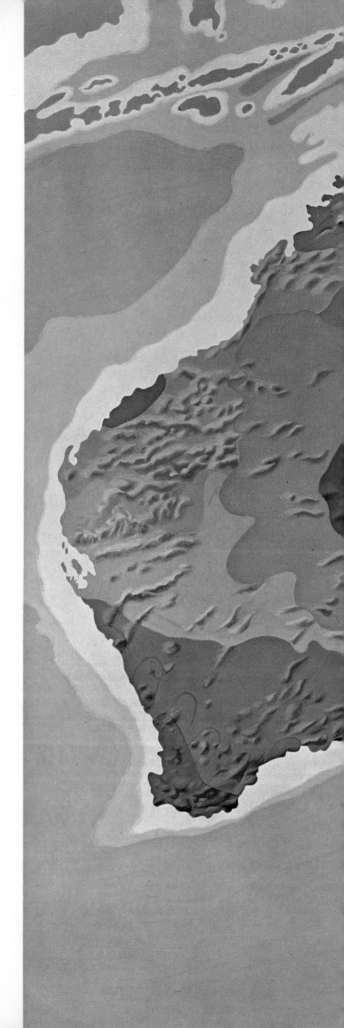

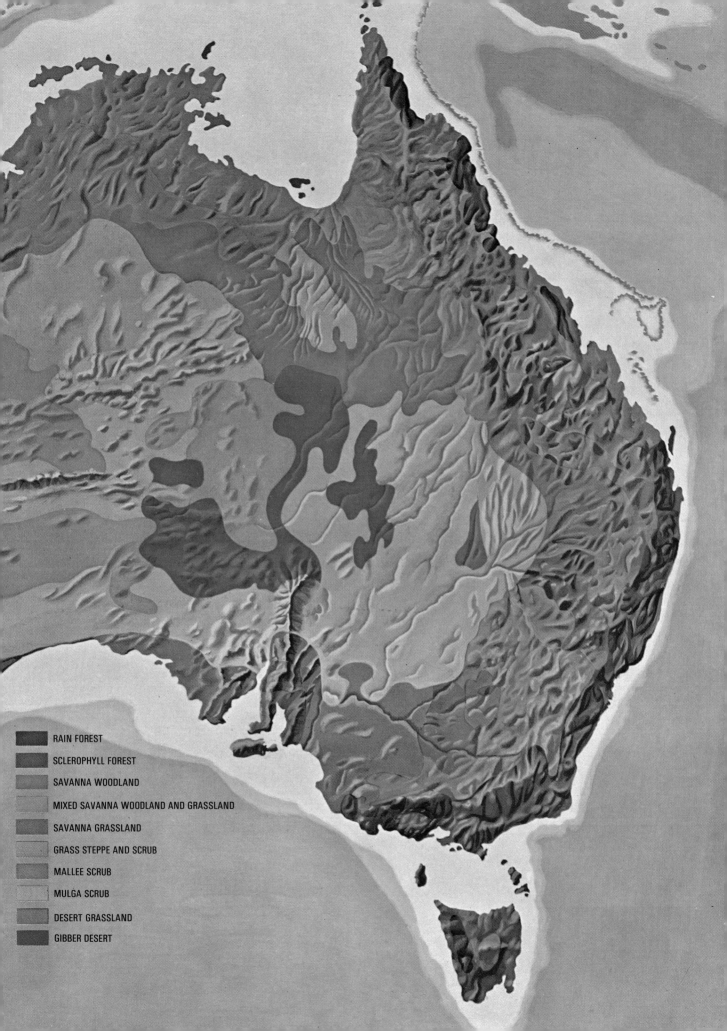

RAIN FOREST

SCLEROPHYLL FOREST

SAVANNA WOODLAND

MIXED SAVANNA WOODLAND AND GRASSLAND

SAVANNA GRASSLAND

GRASS STEPPE AND SCRUB

MALLEE SCRUB

MULGA SCRUB

DESERT GRASSLAND

GIBBER DESERT

The Great Western Plateau

Almost two thirds of Australia swells up as the Great Western Plateau, an uneven platform 600 to more than 2,000 feet above sea level. Though it stretches from the west coast through the Northern Territory and South Australia into Queensland, the plateau is thinly populated; at least three quarters of it has fewer than one inhabitant per eight square miles. It is made up of mesas, buttes, wind-carved cliffs and ranges (*right*), incredibly flat sand plains, undulating sand ridges and around 200 lakes, most of them dry most of the time. There are few rivers worthy of the name, for the rain on much of the plateau amounts to less than 10 inches a year. Everywhere ancient land surfaces and rocks stand revealed, and in the southwest, the foundation of the continent, the more than a billion-year-old shield, crops up in an area bigger than France.

A ROCK OVERHANG frames a stretch of the Great Western Plateau. The vegetation here, as throughout much of the plateau, is mostly drought-resistant mulga scrub.

The Nullarbor Plain

Sweeping in an uninterrupted line to the horizon, the Nullarbor Plain, once the bed of an ancient sea, stands 200 to 400 feet above the waters out of which it rose sometime during the last million years. It parallels around 600 miles of the south coast and rolls back into the continent for 150 miles on a foundation consisting primarily of soft limestone up to 900 feet thick. It is covered with a thin coat of soil and is dotted with saltbush and bluebush, practically the only plants that will grow on it. Rain seeps underground and emerges as springs along the cliffs. Caverns riddle the limestone, and where their roofs have caved in, there are depressions up to three miles wide and 20 feet deep. One of the curiosities of the plain is deep "swallow holes," which lead into the caves. Depending upon barometric conditions, they suck in or expel air.

SAWTOOTH CLIFFS abruptly terminate the Nullarbor Plain at the Great Australian Bight. Stretching 120 miles, they are the longest unbroken cliffs in the world.

THE PEBBLY SURFACE OF A GIBBER PLAIN, ITS MONOTONY BROKEN BY TREES GROWING IN A DRAINAGE CHANNEL, EXTENDS TO THE HORIZON

The Gibber Desert

Of the various kinds of deserts covering the interior of the Australian continent, the most barren by far are the gibber plains. They are thickly mantled with wind-polished stones, round or angular in shape and ranging in size from boulders a foot across to pebbles. These consist of quartzite, jasper, chalcedony—a variety of quartz that is often translu-

cent and beautifully striped—and porcelanite, which looks like unglazed porcelain. They may be a bright red, a reddish brown or reddish purple, and when the sun shines on them, they glitter like little mirrors.

The gibber plains occur in parts of South Australia (above), Western Australia, Queensland and

New South Wales. Formed over the course of millions of years, they represent practically all that remains of an ancient land surface, the rest having been eroded to dust and blown away. The rocks that remained, heating up by day and cooling by night, alternately expanded and contracted, and broke into smaller and smaller pieces. The process continues today, gradually lowering the level of the plains, and can best be observed around the edges of a flat-topped mesa. Here, the wind blowing away the softer, weathered rock forming the sides of the mesa will undercut the hard upper surface. This breaks off and the fallen chunks become gibbers —the aboriginal term for the stones themselves.

23

AYERS ROCK, one of the strange land forms found at the center of the continent, has been furrowed, pocked and polished by the wind. A red sandstone that changes color with the light of the day, it is six miles around, more than a mile and a half long and 1,100 feet high. On its summit, there are basins and at its base, caves. The rock dates back some 230 million years.

The Eastern Highlands

Australia is unique among the continents of the world in that it has no active volcanoes, no year-round snow fields, no glaciers and no high mountains. While the rocks of other continents were undergoing extensive crustal movement, folding and faulting, to become alpine mountain chains, those of Australia experienced relatively little movement. Along the east coast, however, uplifting did take place and is largely responsible for the creation of the Eastern Highlands. These stretch from the tip of northern Queensland to the border of South Australia in a broad belt, and although nowhere especially high, they capture the greater portion of the rain that falls on the continent. In addition to being blessed with fertile soil, the Highlands contain important supplies of lead, silver and gold, as well as some of the world's finest and largest coal deposits.

A 6,000-FOOT-HIGH LAKE fills a basin left by a glacier thousands of years ago. It is but one of several on the upper slopes of the Snowy Mountains, highest range in the Eastern Highlands.

THE STONE BLADES of a formation known as "the breadknife" stick up from slopes in the Warrumbungle Range at the western edge of the Eastern Highlands in New South Wales. Of volcanic origin, the range has other fantastically shaped crests and cliffs, and is the site of a national park. Its aboriginal name, Warrumbungle, is thought to mean "little mountains."

27

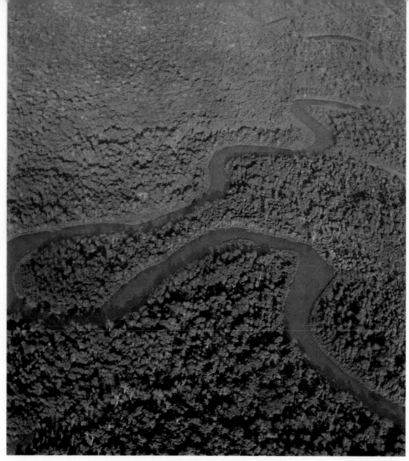

STEAMY JUNGLES covering most of New Guinea's lowlands (*above*) and low-lying slopes (*right*) reflect the hot, wet climate. Most areas get more than eight feet of rain a year.

New Guinea and Tasmania

One hundred miles off northern Australia lies New Guinea; 100 miles off the south coast is Tasmania. Both, of course, are islands (New Guinea is the world's second largest island), both are extremely mountainous, and both get heavy rains the year round. There the comparison ends. New Guinea has a tropical climate, Tasmania a temperate one. Moreover, their mountain chains can be traced to different geological origins. Those of Tasmania represent a continuation of the Eastern Highlands of continental Australia. The mountains of New Guinea are part of the great chain that begins with the Himalayas and sweeps through Southeast Asia and into the Pacific. They extend the length of the island in a swath about 1,500 miles long and 50 to 150 miles wide. Hundreds of them rise 10,000 or more feet above sea level, with the highest, Carstensz, a cloud-scraping 16,000 feet. Many over 5,000 feet are rained on almost constantly, and water running down their steep slopes has led to a complex drainage system. New Guinea's ruggedness has impeded exploration by botanists, and thousands of different plants may yet await discovery there.

GLACIER-SCULPTED, a Tasmanian peak stands reflected in Dove Lake. This and nearby mountains form the roof of Tasmania, a 5,000-foot-high zone on the western side of the island.

New Zealand

Only 1,000 miles long and not quite as big as California, the island country of New Zealand contains many of the great natural wonders of the South Pacific. Mountains stretch the length of this temperate land, and on South Island they rise to alpine heights and are snow-covered the year round. Some are saddled with glaciers *(opposite)*. Along the southwest coast, the mountains drop suddenly to the sea and form steep-walled fiords. On North Island, three volcanoes pile up against the sky and mark the beginning of a 5,000-square-mile area of thermal activity. Around the spa of Rotorua *(left)*, there are, in addition to the fiercely active geysers, boiling pools of mud, bubbling mud pots, blowholes and steaming mineral springs, all arising from cracks that run deep down through the earth's crust.

A JET OF STEAM rises from the ground near Rotorua, center of North Island's thermal district. Maori living close by still cook in hot springs.

A MIRROR FOR THE SKY, Lake Hayes is located in the lake district of South Island. Trees like these golden poplars were introduced by early settlers and light up the landscape in fall.

A RIBBON OF ICE AND SNOW, one of the four glaciers near 12,349-foot-high Mount Cook flows down a craggy slope. Fifteen other peaks in the Southern Alps tower over 10,000 feet.

VARNISHED WITH ICE, snow gums stand outlined against the sky on a mountain in Victoria. Though subject to hard winters at such high altitudes, they follow the evergreen habit of the other eucalypts and keep their leaves the year round.

2

A Long Isolation
and Its Results

THE resident wildlife of a continent is more than a set of branches grown locally from the tree of evolution; it is also an expression of the land itself, written over the ages in adaptive protoplasm. Each living thing—platypus or peony, night crawler or nightingale, kangaroo or katydid—has been shaped partly by the genetic possibilities and limitations of the stock from which it came and partly by the opportunities which the land afforded its forebears. Isolated Australia has offered some unusual possibilities for development, and these are reflected in the unusual character of the wildlife we find there today.

So odd and so oddly assorted are many of the Australian creatures that some of the questions they inevitably pose to scientific minds are still unanswered nearly two centuries after the first reports of them reached Europe. From the time Australia was first discovered, explorers and colonists were struck by the peculiarities of many of the native beasts and remarked on them in letters home. Their accounts seemed so outlandish back in Europe that they reinforced a widespread popular belief that everything on the "down under" side of the world must be topsy-turvy. The scientists of the time, less credulous, tended to the opposite extreme and regarded some of the skins and skeletons sent home for their study as possible fakes, stitched together by the same wily oriental taxi-dermists who had already duped seamen with mermaids compounded out of monkey skins and fishtails.

The more unsettling reports from Australia concerned animals the size of greyhounds that leaped like grasshoppers, swans that were black instead of white, furry "water moles" that had ducklike beaks and were rumored to lay eggs, gigantic birds that could not fly and "foxes" that could. Today these grotesqueries still sound strange, but they are none of them fakes or fancies. We now have names for them and know where they hang on the tree of life. The flying foxes are large fruit bats; the nonflying birds are cassowaries and emus, forms which have exchanged wing power for sureness afoot and bigness of body; the fur-clad egg layers are primitive mammals called platypuses; the swans are ordinary swans in all but their blackness, which is only feather-deep; and of course the leapers are kangaroos, relatives of the American opossum.

THESE creatures, some familiar to zoo-goers, are only the most spectacular inhabitants of the Australasian region. In New Zealand, besides tuataras and kiwis, there are forests full of oddly archaic ferns and tree ferns, and a small motley assortment of insects, frogs and birds which show only the most tenuous family ties to relatives in other parts of the globe. Until the Polynesian Maori less than a thousand years ago brought black rats and dogs to the islands, there were no mammals at all except two species of bat. There were no snakes on New Zealand either, nor are there any today.

More than half of Australia's frogs belong to a single family, the leptodactylids, shared only with South America. In the reptile ranks, more than half the snakes belong to a single venomous family, the front-fanged elapids. At least two of them, the taipan and the tiger snake, vie with the king cobras of India, the mambas of Africa and the bushmasters of South America as the most toxic snakes on earth. The lively lizards of the land split up into several dominant groups ranging from queer little wriggling snake-lizards to alligator-sized monitors 10 feet long that bellow like bulls and, when excited, are said to gallop about on their hind legs. Bird life, too, is characterized by a number of different burgeoning groups. Besides emus and cassowaries, there are melodious lyrebirds, dancing bowerbirds, mound-building megapodes, exquisite birds of paradise and as gaudy a gabble of parrots as can be found on earth. In Australia even the boneless small fry can be breathtaking. Some of the earthworms, for instance, measure a couple of yards long when contracted and as much as 10 feet long when they are extending themselves.

THE ANCIENT SHAPING OF AUSTRALIA

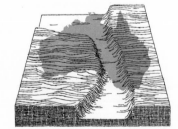 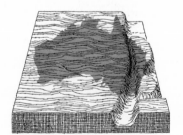 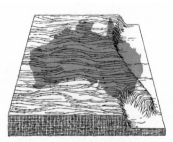

CAMBRIAN

These drawings show the probable shape of Australia during the past, with its modern outline superimposed in color for scale. Five to six hundred million years ago, Australia looked like this: a huge land mass split in two by a shallow sea.

SILURIAN

During the Silurian, about 405 million years ago, the sea moved to the east, forming large islands off the coast. This sea remained shallow; in fact, during the entire geologic history of Australia, it probably never exceeded 600 feet in depth.

DEVONIAN

By 345 million years ago, crustal movements had all but eliminated the sea. Volcanic activity and mountain building occurred in the east. Corals and shells left limestone deposits on the floor of the sea—some visible aboveground today.

Australia's mammals are even more distinctive than its plants and lower animals. Whereas in other lands the mammals are entirely or predominantly placentals, which produce their young in a fairly complete, fully formed condition, the most characteristic of Australian mammals are either monotremes, which lay eggs, or marsupials, which give birth to partially developed, almost embryonic young ones. Before the coming of man, there were about 108 native placental mammal species in Australia and these were all bats or rats and mice. By comparison there were more than 120 marsupials and two egg-laying monotremes, the platypus and spiny anteater.

The only marsupials surviving outside of Australasia today are the small opossums and smaller caenolestoids, or "opossum rats," of South, Central and North America. Fossils indicate, however, that they once ranged from North America to Europe, where they died out only about 25 million years ago. Of whatever land or age, all marsupials share a common and awkward peculiarity in their means of reproduction. Lacking a well-developed womb and placenta—the amazing membrane through which the mother's body provides the embryo with abundant nourishment and oxygen—the marsupial mother cannot give her young ones a long, safe time of internal growth. At birth, each fetus, proceeding under its own power, must climb instinctively through forests of maternal fur until it either loses its way and perishes or reaches a clearing on the abdomen where the milk-giving nipples stand. On most marsupials, the clearing is canopied by a pouch of skin, and it is here in this substitute for a womb that the young one—provided it creeps in safely and can find an unoccupied teat—completes the development which advanced mammals have already put behind them when they are born.

In contrast to American opossums, the 117 Australian marsupial species now come in many forms and sizes and fill an entire range of habitats with their styles of living. Some move through branches with the aid of their prehensile tails, as South American monkeys do. Some live on the ground like field mice. Some scamper up trunks like squirrels or parachute down from high limbs like flying squirrels. One tiny blind thing, *Notoryctes*, tunnels in the ground like a mole and looks so much like the golden mole of South Africa that superficially the two are almost indistinguishable. Another, the numbat, has a long snout and an extensile tongue like an anteater's, specialized for preying on termites and ants. The wombat roots and grazes for a living and resembles a marmot or capybara. The cuscus lazes and browses with the sluggishness of a sloth. So does that living, breathing image of a child's Teddy bear, the koala.

PERMIAN

About 250 million years ago, the east-west dimensions of the continent were shrunk to what they are today. During the early Permian, the land was glaciated, but with a gradual warming of climate, lush vegetation began to appear.

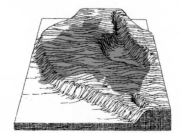

JURASSIC

During the Jurassic, 180 to 135 million years ago, heavy rains filled low-lying regions, enormous fresh-water lakes were formed, and the sandstone that holds the reservoir underlying the Great Artesian Basin today was laid down at this time.

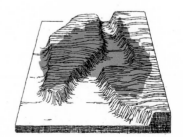

CRETACEOUS

The Cretaceous, 135 to 63 million years ago, saw a return of the sea, which separated east from west. But in the millions of years that followed, the sea dried up, coastal areas sank and Australia gradually emerged in its present outline.

There are pouched "cats," "tiger cats," a "wolf" and even a scavenger known as the Tasmanian devil. Less than a million years ago, there was a pouched "lion," *Thylacoleo*, now extinct, and also, within memory of the Stone Age human aborigines, *Diprotodon*, a buck-toothed animal the size of a rhinoceros, which grazed in groups on the western plains. Today the largest marsupials are still plant eaters. These are those spooky, irrepressible creatures, the kangaroos.

Describing all these extraordinary animals was difficult enough; relating them in an evolutionary way to forms known elsewhere was a great and fascinating task. But the third and biggest problem was and still is to account for Australian wildlife in terms of the past—to decide where the root stocks came from and when: in short, to reconstruct the evolutionary history of Australia and fit it into the evolutionary history of the earth.

The broad problem of accounting for Australian wildlife hinges, to a large extent, on the problem of accounting for the group of mammals so peculiarly characteristic of this continent—the marsupials. When did they arrive in Australia? Why have they subdivided there? What do they tell us about the continent's remote past? These questions are fraught with conjecture and controversy. But the various theories which have been offered to answer them are fascinating and they all agree on one point: Australia, in developing its present fauna and physical make-up, has followed a distinctive course of its own.

THE very first marsupials and the very first placentals both evolved at about the same time, from a single root stock of primitive reptilian mammals, the pantotheres, which flourished some 135 million years ago in the World Continent, the periodically interconnected land masses of the Northern Hemisphere. The first actual fossils of both marsupials and placentals, found in Europe and North America, date from somewhat later, from the second half of the Cretaceous, 100 to 63 million years ago, but their descent from the pantotheres is believed certain. At this time, the marsupials outnumbered the placentals. This fact, plus certain primitive features in their anatomy, suggests that they split from the pantothere stock earlier and enjoyed an earlier success. It is as if the mammals went into production with an early model—the marsupials—while the placentals were still experimenting, perfecting their elaborate internal reproductive system and developing the habits and structures to go with it.

After this beginning, the history of marsupials is not the same in the different continents. In South America all wildlife was isolated about 60 million years ago by the disappearance of the land bridges to the North American continent. Thus a group of primitive marsupials and primitive placentals survived there in isolation and developed side by side until the emergence of the Panamanian land bridge two or three million years ago. Then they were swamped by a horde of new creatures which invaded from the north. Before this happened, all the large South American grazing animals were placentals and all the large meat eaters were marsupials.

Why did not a similar situation prevail in Australia? Why are there no primitive placentals such as shrews, hedgehogs or pangolins in residence there? Why should the only indigenous terrestrial placentals be rodents, a group which did not begin spreading on earth until a mere 25 million years ago?

To answer these key questions, naturalists assume that Australia, at some time in the Cretaceous between 63 and 135 million years ago, must have been linked to the World Continent. This link may have been an isthmus or a chain of islands. In either case, certain deductions can be drawn from the relative lack of placentals in Australia. If the linkage was an isthmus, it must have sunk before the placentals became numerous enough to take advantage of it. If the linkage was an island arc, then the straits separating the islands must somehow have been more easily negotiated by the marsupials, which crossed in greater numbers, than by the placentals, which were largely excluded.

How this may have worked nobody knows, but there are several interesting theories on the subject. The simplest and most probable, advanced by the paleontologist George Gaylord Simpson, combines logic and chance. It assumes that a small, tree-dwelling animal would have a better chance of surviving a voyage on a piece of driftwood torn loose in a storm than would a larger, ground-dwelling creature. Whether such an animal would be a placental or marsupial type would be a matter of pure chance—but in any event, chance would favor the more numerous of the two groups, and this may well have been marsupial at the time when the first emigrations to Australia took place. The element of chance gains added credence when one considers the immense periods of time and the thousands of animals involved—just as a dice player has a much better chance of throwing double sixes three times in a row if he has 10,000 throws to do it in than if he has only 10 throws.

Certainly, no water gap is so wide that it can keep out all life. The odd assortments of snails, insects, reptiles and plants found on remote Pacific islands, thousands of miles from any continental land, testify unmistakably to the fact that every now and then in the spaciousness of geologic time a wind-lofted seed or a pregnant female adrift on a flood-torn tangle of underbrush may carry its species across immense expanses of ocean.

On the basis of present geography, the obvious place to look for a past connection between Australia and the World Continent is in the New Guinea region. Geologists have collected evidence which indicates that from time to time since the Permian there have been connections between Australia and New Guinea, although evidence for a connection between New Guinea and the World Continent is still lacking. The most important period in the history of the Australian marsupials was at the end of the Cretaceous period some 70 million years ago. It is easy to conclude that this was the time when the marsupials made their entrance; that they came down a peninsula out of Asia and crossed an unknown number of straits to reach another peninsula hooking up out of Australia through New Guinea toward the northwest. Along with the marsupials presumably came other animals—possibly birds of a type that might have fathered the emus and cassowaries, some of the peculiar Australian lizards and frogs—and plants, notably the myrtles to which the eucalypts belong.

Most naturalists are convinced that some such Late Cretaceous emigration from the World Continent actually did take place, that is to say, that the major colonization at this time was from the north. But there are also several groups of dissenters who are fascinated by the perplexing fact that certain primitive plants and animals in the Australian region are most closely related to similar forms surviving in South America and, to a lesser degree, in Africa. The orthodox explanation is that certain forms, global in spread, have survived only in the southern dead ends of the earth where they were farthest from the competitive heartlands of the World Continent. But another, more startling and hotly disputed interpretation is that the southern continents—at a time when the world was warm—were connected and accessible to each other across what we know today as Antarctica.

This connection, forming a single Antarctic supercontinent, was envisaged first by 19th Century geologists. They found evidence that one group of plants, dominated by a seed fern called *Glossopteris*, overran so much of the Southern Hemisphere some 250 million years ago that their abundance could be explained only by such a fusion of all the southern land masses. This supercontinent was given the name of Gondwanaland. Some thought that Gondwanaland remained intact until about 100 million years ago, thus accounting for the presence of marsupials in South America and Australia. Others, if they believed it at all, said it must have disintegrated earlier, and conceded that the marsupials must have come in from Asia according to the orthodox view. To confuse the issue still more, a German meteorologist, Alfred Wegener, suggested in 1912 that *all* the continents, both northern and southern, once abutted each other and have since somehow drifted apart to their present stations.

SCIENTISTS today treat all these early speculations warily, but one striking piece of evidence gives new life to the theory of continental drift and suggests that it may deserve attention after all. When lava cools or sediments are compacted to make rock, magnetizable minerals in them line up in the direction of the earth's magnetic field. Theoretically, therefore, rock strata of any given geological period will show where the magnetic poles lay at that time. As a practical matter, the assemblage of a great deal of evidence by geologists indicates that the fossil magnets in the rocks of the various continents by and large do agree as to where the magnetic poles were at any one time. In Australia, however, the geological compass is off. Minerals in rocks known to be from 93 million to 200 million years old point to a south magnetic pole that is not in the same place as the pole indicated by fossil magnetism elsewhere.

The discrepancy can be explained in two ways. Either the earth itself at that time was nondipolar—i.e. had no magnetic poles at all or had more than the two it has now—or Australia itself has moved, drifting north as much as 3,000 miles in the last 100 million years. The first explanation is difficult for some geophysicists to accept. The second explanation is equally difficult for paleontologists to swallow: it seems highly unlikely to them that Australia could have become a home for thousands of kinds of animals while drifting north from the Antarctic Ocean. Therefore, throughout the rest of this book it will be assumed that the theory of marsupial emigration from the north is the right one, but all readers are hereby advised to keep the other possibilities in mind.

In addition to being isolated as a unit from the rest of the world, the parts of modern Australia are also isolated from one another. Each of the island outposts of the continent—New Zealand, New Guinea and the smaller islands—has its own plants and animals which are distinct from, yet similar to, those of the mainland. New Zealand, for instance, has peculiar fauna—including frogs, which could not possibly have traveled over the sea—that almost demand a former direct land connection with the continent. Did Australia and New Zealand once lie closer together and then drift apart? Did a continuous arc of land, or islands, once extend from Australia through New Guinea to New Caledonia and Fiji, from there following a submarine ridge; or did a now-lost land mass occupy the Tasman Sea? Some of the older geologists inclined toward the latter view, citing evidence found not only in the rocks of the islands but also in the floors of the Coral and Tasman seas. They have postulated a continent that was a sister of Australia and which they named Tasmantis. It was even suggested that Tasmantis foundered only 10 to 20 million years ago. However, if this were so, there should be marsupial and monotreme remains in New Zealand, since these animals were plentiful in Australia much earlier than that. But since none have been found, it seems more reasonable to believe that if Tasmantis existed at all, it did so in the heyday of the tuatara's ancestors 200 million years ago.

Australia itself began to form more than 1,500 million years ago. Its first nuclei of continental granite thrust their heads above seas barely stirring with microscopic forms of life. Precambrian fossils show jellyfish, segmented worms and other forms of life in Australia more than 600 million years old. Vascular land plants—plants with erect stems and tubes in them to carry up water—are known first from Silurian fossils laid down on Australian shores more than 400 million years ago. But after this early Australian preeminence, the whole region down under, from a zoological point of view, seems to have lapsed into a period of relative inactivity. Other nuclei of continental granite emerging to the north in the World Continent formed a larger, more prosperous stage for evolution, and in them the main drama was played. The great breakthroughs in land life —from fish to amphibian to reptile to bird and mammal, or from moss to fern to conifer to hardwood tree and flowering plant—all of these are thought to have been achieved on the World Continent. Ancient Australia, as far as we know now, seems to have remained off stage, receiving outcasts and giving them a place to survive and diversify, but probably did not cradle any radically new forms of life on its own.

As elsewhere in the world, land plants in Australia developed before land animals, and for millions of years after they put in their first appearance in the Silurian, the Australasian region shared with the rest of the continents a stately succession of floras which gradually clothed the land ever more luxuriantly in vegetation. Far from being the arid land it is for the most part today, Australia grew green with brakes of ferns. These gave way to jungles of seed ferns and cycads, and these in turn were succeeded by aromatic forests of conifers. The fossil record, though admittedly incomplete, shows few traces of the large animal life which elsewhere in the world was characteristic of such woodlands—only a few score relics have been unearthed of amphibians, dinosaurs and other terrestrial reptiles. In the oceans, fishes left plentiful fossils in marine sediments, and Australia had one gigantic marine reptile, a stocky-necked plesiosaur that appears to have been unique to the continent. This monster, dubbed *Kronosaurus queenslandicus*, had a toothy skull nine feet long and probably a bulkier body than any reptile that ever lived.

T HE Late Cretaceous and Tertiary saw the final stage in the shaping of the world as we know it—the time of the great mountain-building. Intermittently the earth trembled, spouted out lava and wrinkled up in mountain folds, changing the face of the planet radically. In many places shallow, island-studded seas receded to lay bare continental land masses, and temperatures and rainfall changed. It seems likely that provincial regions in both land and sea were opened up to one another, pitting one pocket of evolution against another, leading to widespread extinctions. Not only the dinosaurs, but also the great marine ichthyosaurs and plesiosaurs, the flying reptilian pterosaurs, and several mollusk and plant lines all vanished together. The extermination of hitherto successful forms was so marked that naturalists have sought all manner of ingenious reasons—from microbes to cosmic rays—to explain it. But the accepted explanation remains as it has for a century: that changing temperatures and rainfall patterns, rising lands and wrenching confrontations be-

**AN EXTINCT
AUSTRALIAN GIANT**

Kronosaurus, the largest flesh-eating marine reptile known, swam in the sea that covered much of Australia 100 million years ago. It was 42 feet long and had a nine-foot head. It belonged to a group known as plesiosaurs, many of which had snaky necks and whose remains are found scattered over the world, but Kronosaurus fossils occur only in Australia.

THE EUCALYPTUS EXPLOSION

Few groups of trees have diversified more spectacularly than the eucalypts, which, in the course of perhaps 50 million years, have evolved into over 600 species. They grow throughout most of their native Australia, as well as in New Guinea.

MOUNTAIN ASH   RIVER RED GUM

The largest Eucalyptus is the mountain ash. Second in size only to the giant sequoias of California, the mature trees may have a trunk 300 feet or more in height with a diameter of six to nine feet. The most widespread Eucalyptus is the river red gum, a 120-foot-tall specimen of which is shown here. It usually lives along rivers and on periodically inundated flood plains, and tolerates climates ranging from tropical to temperate.

tween evolutionary recluses and newcomers were enough over a few millions of years to wreak the havoc that took place.

For Australia, a small, temperate continent, a flat, ancient continent, a continent that had gone without benefit of great mountain-building and expansion, the Late Cretaceous land rise took place largely off stage, with few major geologic consequences. The shallow seas that at one time subdivided it into at least three separate land masses withdrew their arms and the eastern seaboard began a slow uplift, culminating in peaks that today stand over 6,000 feet high.

The zoological consequences, on the other hand, were profound. If there were any surviving dinosaurs, they did not live to enjoy the epochs of isolation which followed. Instead, Cretaceous marsupials and flowering plants, with infinite slowness, spread out and made the land their own. After their coming, the island arcs to the north apparently subsided, preventing further sizable immigrations until rodents began to trickle in about 25 million years later.

S INCE the beginning of the Oligocene epoch about 35 million years ago, a procession of modern rodents, lizards, snakes, birds and plants has come down from the north and effected a transformation of the old Australian flora and fauna. Many of the ancient species were probably crowded out, even as some of Australia's indigenous creatures in modern times have been driven to the verge of extinction by imports from Europe. Those that survived, as well as the most tenacious of the immigrants, in obedience to evolution's basic law adapted themselves, fitting into and exploiting a variety of niches. And, in time, two factors worked primarily to shape the oddly assorted species we know now— two factors peculiar to Australia and its adjacent islands: isolation and, ultimately, aridity.

In parts of Australia, aridity is a relatively recent phenomenon. We know from fossil evidence that over most of south central Australia, where only grass and scrub grow now, there used to sprawl a luxuriant subantarctic rain forest of southern beech trees, threaded by majestic rivers which piled up deep layers of sediment beneath the beds now long since dry. The change from beech to eucalypt and acacia took place during the Pliocene. Subsequently, the Pleistocene was characterized by reasonably good conditions and north-south movements of the climatic belts. Big marsupials, including *Diprotodons*, *Notatheriums* and *Euryzygemas*, all now extinct, grazed or browsed in numbers on the plains. *Livistona* palms must have ranged through parts of the interior, for an isolated grove of them survives today in the Macdonnell Ranges, hundreds of miles from their nearest kin on the coast. They could not have reached the area other than by a former direct distribution through what is now desert.

There would appear to be no doubt that, in southern Australia at least, all this lushness ended quite abruptly. The land dried up, forests retreated, rivers vanished and some of the last *Diprotodons* perished flank to flank in the evaporating waters of lakes. At the same time, glaciers which periodically had spread around the mountaintops of Tasmania and the southeast once again shrank dramatically. The time of this great change has been fixed by scientists using various dating techniques, and all agree that it coincided roughly with the time, about 10,000 years ago, when the huge continental glaciers of the last ice age withdrew in the Northern Hemisphere.

This is the sort of relatively sudden and drastic change that is likely to mean inevitable extinction for many species; and indeed, Australia lost its share of plants and animals which could not adapt to a life of dryness. Yet others—and large numbers of species of them—are so well adapted to extremes of aridity in Australia today that the continent is a veritable showcase for life in arid regions. Ten thousand years seems too short a time to produce so many drought-adapted native species—acacias, eucalypts, desert lizards and frogs, to name only the most obvious ones. How could this have happened?

It probably lies in the simple fact that Australia has always had areas of aridity which, depending on the general climate, moved north or south through the various periods of geologic time. Since most parts of the continent were at various times quite wet, it seems reasonable to suppose that elsewhere there were dry areas—that Australia, for at least the last 10 or 20 million years, has always had some desert proving grounds where the ancestors of the drought-adapted plants and animals which now people the outback were able to evolve.

Today the principal plant and animal communities of Australia are roughly delineated by the critical precipitation lines on a weather map. In a broad sense, these rainfall belts zone the various kinds of plant formation: the most drought-adapted ones in the gibber and desert grassland of the center, surrounded almost entirely by those of the mulga and steppe, which are surrounded in turn—almost like a series of concentric ellipses—by a belt of mallee and savanna woodland and, on the wettest coasts in the east and southwest, by the flourishing trees of full-fledged forest.

Each of these different plant communities provides different opportunities to animals—different amounts of cover, different nesting facilities and, most important, different kinds of prey animals, leaves, seeds and flowers to eat. As a result, many species of Australian animals, particularly of insects and birds, are indirectly zoned and limited in distribution by the rainfall belts because they depend on specific plant communities for a livelihood. A honey possum living in the moist coastal woods of southwestern Australia will never come face to face with its cousin, the eastern pygmy possum, which inhabits a similar environment on the east coast—for a thousand miles of desert separate the two and they have had to go down separate evolutionary paths.

Some idea of the relative importance of the arid zones in Australia can be gained by comparing the areas occupied by the various plant formations. The patches of rain forest on the east coast cover less than 1 per cent of the total continental area. The dense *Eucalyptus* forests of the wet east and southwest occupy about 7 per cent. The open savanna forests fringing the interior account for about 24 per cent. Steppe or savanna fills 6 per cent. Mulga preempts a huge 30 per cent, and mallee 7 per cent. Desert grass tussocks or sterile gibber take up some 14 per cent. The remaining 1 per cent or more belongs to mangroves and miscellaneous swamp, marsh and bog formations.

In a broad way Australian zoologists have been able to recognize four distinctive regions of fauna: the northeast and north, the southeast, the center and the southwest. The animals of the center, living in arid, open country, are distinctive because of their adaptations to harsh surroundings. Those of the southwest are even more distinctive because they have long been evolving on their own, isolated from the rest of the continent by the desert belt. This region of the southwest also has a larger percentage of endemic plant species than any other part of Australia. It has over 6,000 species—as rich a temperate flora as any in the world. Here, as elsewhere in Australia, all these various species have sprung from only a few native groups, spreading out and diversifying to occupy a range of niches which anywhere else in the world would be occupied by a far

COOLABAH

One of the hardiest of the eucalypts, the coolabah grows in the dry interior of New South Wales, Queensland and Western Australia, where it withstands frosts, and temperatures as high as 120° F. Reaching a height of 80 feet, it yields a dense wood that weighs 89 pounds per cubic foot and is used for railroad ties.

SNOW GUM

A cold-tolerant Eucalyptus, the snow gum grows on seasonally snow-covered mountain slopes and ridges from 2,000 to 5,000 feet high. It can withstand 50 to 100 frosts a year. Here it is shown as a 30-foot-tall, wind-deformed specimen, though it takes other shapes and, in sheltered places, reaches up to over 60 feet.

THE TWO-FACED EUCALYPTUS LEAF

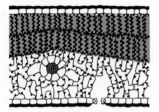

APPLE LEAF

Unlike the leaves of most deciduous trees, which spread out horizontally and receive the sun's rays on their upper surfaces, the leaves of most Eucalyptus trees dangle straight down and get sunlight on both sides. The internal structure of the Eucalyptus leaf is adapted to take advantage of this. Instead of having a single layer of photosynthetic palisade cells, as in ordinary leaves (colored area in cross section above), the Eucalyptus has two palisade layers (cross section below)—and under the microscope looks almost like two ordinary leaves pasted together. In addition, it has stomata (openings for the exchange of gases) on both of its sides, whereas conventional leaves have them only on the bottom.

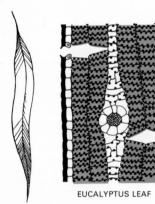

EUCALYPTUS LEAF

greater number of floral and faunal groups. To cite a particularly striking example: three out of four individual trees growing in Australia today belong to one or another of the *Eucalyptus* species.

Today Australia still offers an unrivaled field laboratory for the inquiring zoologist, one which still offers great opportunities for further exploration. However, it must also be said that much of its distinctive wildlife is in serious danger. Australia today is in a situation comparable to that faced by South America two or three million years ago when its long isolation from North America was ended. Just as a parade of advanced placental mammals streaming down across the Panamanian land bridge then decimated the ranks of South American species, so today an influx of foreign mammals is seriously threatening Australia's marsupials. Though no isthmus has provided a bridge for a full-scale invasion, the ancient sea walls of the continent have been effectively breached by ships and airplanes, and the depredations of the invaders have been, in some instances, extreme.

The influx of foreign flora and fauna began in a small way some 25,000 years ago when the human ancestors of the Australian aborigines arrived from the north. It later swelled when the aborigines imported an early breed of domestic dog, now running wild and known as the dingo. Not until the coming of white settlers, however, did the slaughter begin in earnest. In the two centuries since then—a mere second in the workings of nature—the resident evolutionary recluses have been driven to the wall.

Thus a government-sponsored census of the animals in 1963 shows that six out of 123 Australian and Tasmanian marsupials are extinct and 28 more so nearly so that they have not been seen for years. In the past, they were shot and poisoned as pests and for their skins. The land has been drastically altered; forests have been felled for timber, rabbits and sheep have overrun and deteriorated some of the best savannas and grasslands, leaving habitats cut up into corridors and pockets.

ACCORDING to some pessimists, the clash between native and imported forms of life in Australia is likely to end in almost total extermination of the defenders. Others disagree. Rabbits and the prickly-pear cactus have both been brought under control, one by a virus that causes the rabbit disease myxomatosis, and the other by a blight, cactoblastis. Stringent laws now protect many of Australia's characteristic species. The conservationists who have expended some of their best efforts on these measures naturally hold high hopes that they can now preserve the bulk of the marsupial population. But the communities of life which constituted the virgin Australian wilderness have already been altered radically, and the tide of human settlement is flooding, not ebbing.

Though the thought may seem cold-blooded, this process of extinction is itself an important and fascinating object of study. The great dyings of the past—the disappearance of the mighty dinosaurs, for instance—have been recorded with cryptic abruptness in the graven tablets of the earth's crust. No one knows precisely why whole groups of plants and animals periodically vanish or what factors are most significant in conferring superiority to one species over another. Large-scale extinctions, however, usually seem to result whenever two pockets of evolution are opened up to one another after long isolation. For this reason Australasia offers modern science the chance of an eon—a confrontation between native creatures and outsiders which, in its continental scope, is not likely to be matched in tens of millions of years.

A TROPICAL RAIN FOREST ALONG AUSTRALIA'S EAST COAST OFFERS A STRIKING CONTRAST TO THE SPARSE VEGETATION OF THE DRY INTERIOR

Australia's Plants

Though anciently related to plants elsewhere, the flora of Australia is, for the most part, unique. Evolving in isolation for millions of years, it radiated dramatically and is marked by a preponderance of certain types and a dearth of others. The myrtles, for example, are represented by over 600 different Eucalyptus trees and a variety of smaller flowering plants; the conifers by only 36 species.

BLACK WATTLE

BOTTLE TREE

Trees with a Difference

The effect of millions of years of geographical isolation upon the plants shows up conspicuously in the individual look and curious adaptations of many Australian trees. The graceful casuarinas, or she-oaks, have needlelike branchlets that serve as leaves, the leaves themselves being little more than tiny tri-

TEAK, LONE REMNANT OF A RAIN FOREST

GRASS TREE

DESERT CASUARINA

GRAY MANGROVE

PANDANUS

angular scales ringing the branchlets. In some species, there are male and female trees. The grass trees, distantly related to the lilies, grow grassy leaves three or more feet long and put up spikes on which white flowers bloom, usually after brush fires. Bottle trees resemble bottles of all kinds and sizes, and some grow trunks that are six feet around. The acacias, or wattles, show their relationship to peas by producing pods. They number about 600 species, take many shapes and live in a wide range of habitats. Along with the casuarinas and the eucalypts, they are the only hardwoods to have successfully invaded deserts.

A STAND OF BLACKBUTT, A EUCALYPT OF SOUTHEAST SLOPES

The Ubiquitous Eucalypts

Of the trees native to Australia, none are more numerous than the aromatic eucalypts, or gums. Bearing such odd names as the tuart, the bastard box, the red tingle, the coolabah, the maalok, or moort, the bimbil and the wandoo, they number over 600 species and dominate 95 per cent of the forests. Among them is the world's tallest hardwood, the mountain ash, which soars 300 or more feet into the air. At the opposite end of the scale are the dwarf eucalypts, or mallees, scrubby, drought-resistant trees which stand from 10 to 30 feet high.

Characterized uniformly by their thick-skinned, pungent-smelling leaves, the eucalypts show an array of adaptations to climates ranging from tropical to temperate. They grow in deserts, at the edges of rain forests and in swamps, on wind-swept slopes and in sheltered valleys; some root themselves in fertile loam, others in inhospitable sand or hard-packed clay. Because of their hardiness, fast growth rate and valuable timber, oil and resin, many have been introduced abroad. Eucalypts now flourish in regions as far away from Australia as California and Florida, South Africa and South America.

SMOOTH-BARKED RIVER RED GUMS, mirrored in a flooded creek near Alice Springs, are the most widespread of the eucalypts. Growing in regions of low rainfall, where few other

trees can live, they generally line rivers and streams or cluster on flood-inundated plains. As an adaptation to the hot, dry climate, river reds put down two sets of roots. One spreads out in horizontal layers to absorb moisture available near the surface; the other must often penetrate five or more feet of tightly packed clay to reach supplies of underground water.

47

STRIPS OF BARK PEEL FROM THE TRUNK AND CLING TO THE FORKED BRANCHES OF A EUCALYPT BELONGING TO THE STRINGYBARK GROUP

The Telltale Bark

A way of identifying the more than 600 species of eucalypts is by their bark, which may be smooth, like that of the ghost gum opposite, rough and fibrous or hard and deeply furrowed. Many eucalypts shed their outer bark in flakes, ribbons or sheets. Some shed it only part way down the trunk; thus a mountain ash may wear a 50-foot-long stocking of dark, old bark, with as many or more feet of newer, lighter-colored bark showing above. Some shed so much bark that forest floors become littered with it. An acre of mature manna gums will pile 50 tons on the ground. Shedding usually takes place in warm weather, and this poses a fire hazard. During high winds in 1939, glowing ribbons of snow gum bark blew down from mountains into Canberra, 15 miles away, and started blazes in the city.

BLOODWOOD BARK, shown half peeled, cracks into squarish pieces. A red gum often oozes from lesions in the bark—thus the name bloodwood.

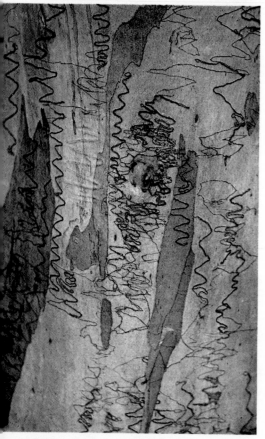

SCRIBBLY GUM gets its name from "scribbles" in its bark and trunk made by insect larvae. The bark flakes off, giving the tree its mottled look.

A GHOST GUM shows the reason for its name—its smooth bark is pure white. Growing throughout northern Australia, it also crops up as a solitary tree in the center, where it is the subject of many aboriginal paintings.

Eucalyptus Flowers— All Stamens and No Petals

The eucalypts, unlike most other plants, shed their petals before they put out their flowers. This happens because the petals are fused and form a protective cap over the maturing bud. As the flower inside expands, the cap of petals splits open and

FORREST'S MARLOCK BEGINNING TO BLOOM

eventually drops off. The word eucalypt refers to the petal cap and is derived from the Greek for well-covered. What is left after the petals are gone is a bunch of stamens—hence the pompon look of the colorful varieties shown on these pages. Later the stamens themselves drop off and the seed capsule comes into full view. These come in many shapes —eggs, tops, cups—and can be as beautiful as the blossoms themselves. Often they are found clinging to branches long after the seeds have dropped out.

LARGE-FRUITED MALLEE IN FLOWER AND IN BUD

WOODWARD'S BLACKBUTT

RED-FLOWERED MALLEE

SPIKE WATTLE

ALPINE GREVILLEA

ORANGE BANKSIA

HONEYSUCKLE

MYRTLES

ONE-SIDED BOTTLE BRUSH

CRIMSON HONEY-MYRTLE

An Australian Flower Sampler

Australia possesses many of the world's most beautiful flowers, as shown by this sampling from three large groups—the acacias, proteaceae and myrtles. The Australian wattles (*above*) account for nearly three quarters of the world's acacias. Their fluffy yellow or cream-colored blossoms are among the most familiar of the continent's flowers and scent large portions of the country in the spring. The proteaceae (*upper panel, opposite*) are also well represented. Of the 12,000 species comprising this family, more than half are in Australia. Although closely related, the native species often have completely different flowers and foliage.

The Australian myrtles include, in addition to the eucalypts, many smaller flowering trees and plants (*lower panel, opposite*). The dazzling tea trees, or melaleucas, number 120 species and, unlike the eucalypts, their flowers have petals. The 20 callistemons bear blossoms that look like bottle brushes, which explains the common names Australians have given some of them.

ROSEMARY SPIDER FLOWER

WOOLLY BANKSIA

ROSE CONE BUSH

BANK'S GREVILLEA

RED BANKSIA

NEEDLEBUSH

COMMON BOTTLE BRUSH

CRIMSON-FLOWERED TEA TREE

STURT PEA

FALSE SARSAPARILLA

Odd Flowers: Odder Names

The unusualness of Australia's wildflowers is reflected in some of their names—lilly pilly, molucca bramble, cootaminda, willow gee-bung, tuckeroo and crinkle-leaved poison. The kangaroo paw at top right suggests how appropriate such bizarre names can often be. Kangaroo paw is even furry to the touch. It is the official flower of Western Australia, an area long undisturbed by climate changes and

KANGAROO PAW

FRINGED VIOLET

CHRISTMAS BELLS

WOODY CLIMBER

LAMB'S TAIL

invasions of the sea, with a flora exceeded only by the tropics in richness. There also grows the sturt pea (*above*), which springs up from seed after rain to become a full-grown blossoming vine in a few weeks. Among the eastern wildflowers shown here are waratah, a shrub with a blossom the size of a small cabbage, and Christmas bells, which grow in marshes and are collected for decorations in December.

WARATAH

HYACINTH ORCHID

COWSLIP ORCHID

DOUBLE TAILS

The Exquisite Orchids

Orchids, normally associated with the tropics, occur throughout much of Australia. Some dwell on trees in rain forests, others on the ground in eucalypt groves, woodlands and alpine grasslands. As on other continents, they are almost all small, exquisitely marked and colored, and often best appreciated with the aid of a magnifying glass. A few, however, depart strikingly from the norm. One, *Galeola foliata*, grows to great heights, climbing trees in the rain forests of northern New South Wales and Queensland, and has been known to measure 44 feet in length. Two others spend their entire lives underground, the only orchids to do so. One of these, the all-white *Cryptanthemus slateri*, bears self-fertilizing flowers and pokes its pod aboveground only for dispersal of its seeds.

CALADENIA CARIACHILA

PINK ROCK LILY

FLESHY LIP ORCHID

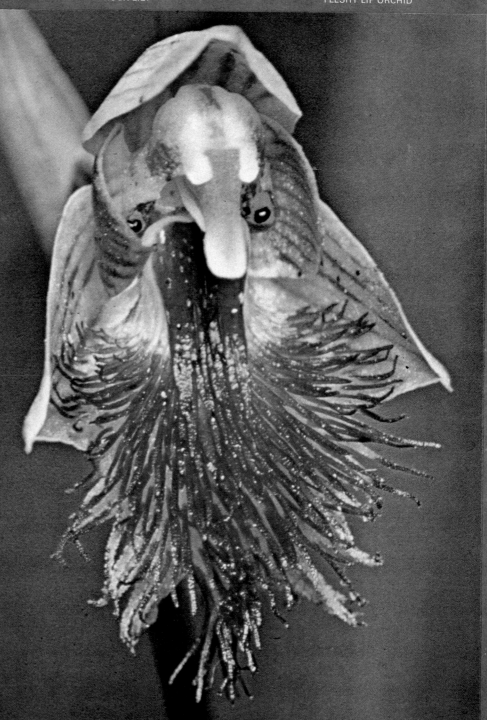

SUN ORCHID

BEARDED ORCHID

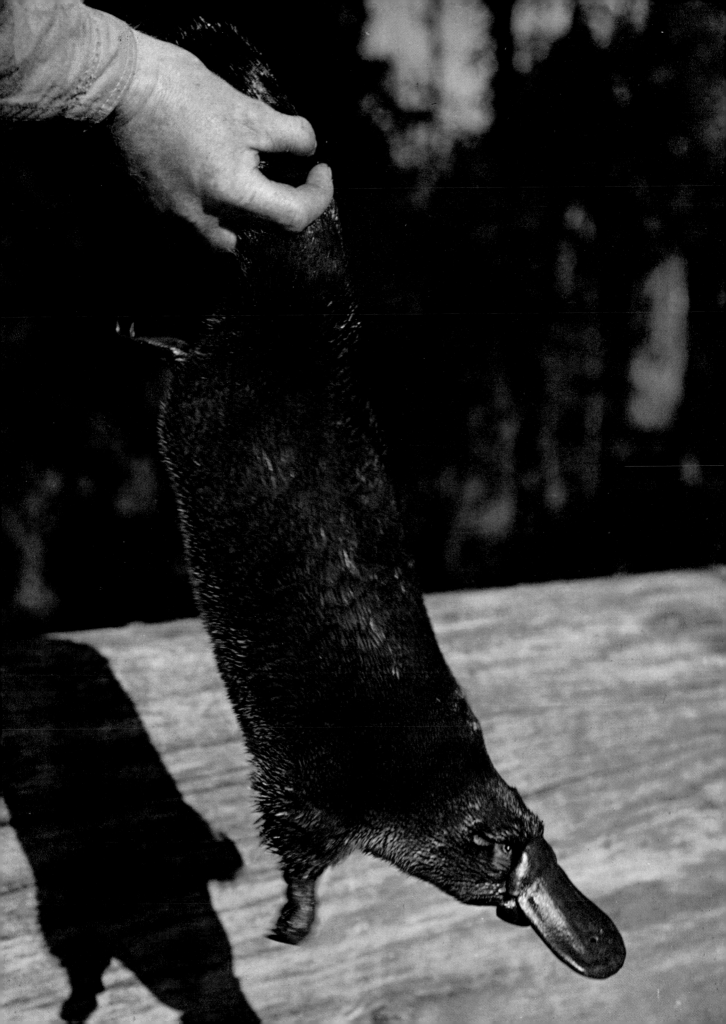

3

Two That
Time Forgot

How has evolution led to intelligent animals with large brains? This is surely one of the most appropriate questions that a human being can ask. And in seeking an answer he will come, sooner or later, to consider a trio of small Australasian beasts: the platypus, *Ornithorhynchus*, and the spiny anteaters, *Tachyglossus* and *Zaglossus*. These out-of-the-way creatures are the most primitive living members of the animal class to which man belongs, the class which has gone furthest in brain development, the mammals.

By definition, mammals are animals that nurse their young. Biologists believe that this nursing and increased maternal care, in conjunction with a gradual increase in the size—and more importantly, in the neural complexity of the brain—have played a significant part in ensuring among the mammals a higher proportion of offspring survival. It is chiefly the neopallium, or cortex, which first appeared as a small new area in reptiles, that enables mammals to profit by experience. This neopallium becomes larger in the monotremes and increasingly prominent in higher mammals until, in man, it overwhelmingly dominates everything else.

In brain, reproduction, skeleton and metabolism, the Australasian monotremes stand at a halfway point between higher mammals and reptiles. Since they are the only known beasts which maintain this level of development, they provide us with a tantalizing keyhole for peering back into the past at our distant mammal forebears. This chapter will be devoted to their appearance as individuals, their anatomical characteristics as a group, their probable ancestry and their possible past history in Australasia.

The most celebrated of the monotremes is the platypus. And surely earth does not harbor a creature more mixed up in outward appearance, or one that has caused more learned perplexity and dispute. Here is a warm-blooded, furry animal that lactates like a mammal, lays eggs like a lizard and dredges food from stream bottoms with a bill that is positively ducklike.

Just to watch a platypus, without knowing anything about its importance as a primitive mammal, is enough to convince anyone of its oddity. As it emerges from its burrow—usually under the roots of a tree by a stream and usually in the half-light of dawn or dusk—its slate-gray bill looks like nothing so much as a leathery sheath which someone has pushed up over its trowel-shaped nose. On the flat upper surface, two small, closely spaced nostrils let in air—and scents and savors. At its upper end, the sheath overlaps the fur of the head in a cufflike fringe. Beyond the fringe, tiny beady eyes gleam from the depths of the fur, set high on the head to enable the animal to scan the banks on either side as well as the sky above for possible dangers. The eyes trail off like commas into dark furrows which are all that can be seen externally of the creature's reptilelike ears. The rest of the head, presenting an air of stolidly directed purpose, flows into the body without any appreciable neck. The fat, flat torso is clothed in an efficient coat of umber-colored fur, coarse on the outside, soft and woolly underneath. Finally, the rear end tapers off into a large flat tail which serves in the water as a combined rudder and stabilizer.

Making for the stream where it finds its food, the platypus waddles on stubby sprawling legs and great five-toed paws heavily webbed for swimming and heavily clawed for digging. As it slides into the water, it unpalms a furl of extra webbing that flaps out beyond the tips of its foreclaws and converts them into veritable frogman flippers. Now it closes its eyes tight, crash dives and heads for the bottom. It blindly nuzzles its way along the mud banks, trusting to its tender nerve-filled bill to feel out prawns and worms, insect larvae and crushable mollusks. In a minute or two, its air is gone and its cheek pouches bulge with food; it surfaces, opens its eyes and warily chews what it has caught. During the course of a night's diving, it will consume in this fashion an incredible quantity of food. The naturalist David Fleay has found that keeping a platypus healthy in captivity takes no fewer than 1,200 earthworms and 50 crayfish every 24 hours, plus additional items such as tadpoles, grubs and beetles.

Early 19th Century biologists could make neither fish, flesh nor fowl of this strange beast. The colonists called it a "duck-mole," passed on seemingly wild stories from the aborigines about its laying eggs, conducted a lively traffic in rugs stitched out of its soft pelts and sent home pickled specimens for the savants of Europe to marvel at, mull over and argue about. In 1802 the surgeon Everard Home found that the "structure of the female organs is unlike anything hitherto met with in quadrupeds." He therefore assigned the duckbill to a new class "intermediate . . . between . . . Mammalia, Aves and Amphibia." At about the same time, a celebrated French naturalist, Étienne Geoffroy Saint-Hilaire, dissected the reproductive organs of a female platypus and came up with the startling opinion that they were those of an egg layer. Jean de Lamarck, the early French proponent of evolution, shared this view but pointed out that the platypus was not a lizard either, because it had a fully developed four-chambered heart; nor was it a bird, because it had no wings and its lungs were set off by a diaphragm in the fashion of mammals. Finally, by definition, the animal could not properly be called a mammal because the female had no mammae—no teats with which to suckle its young. Lamarck astutely classified the creature as "Prototheria," or prototype mammal.

Many platypus pelts later, in 1824, a German anatomist, Johann Friedrich Meckel, discovered that the female duckbill did have tiny milk-giving apertures scattered like so many sweat pores over a small area on her abdomen. Thus, if not a fully fledged mammal, she at least had mammalian tendencies. Whether she also laid eggs remained a hotly debated question for six decades in the natural history museums of Europe. At last, in 1884, a young English zoologist, W. H. Caldwell, sailed out to Australia and saw for himself. In a pregnant platypus which he shot by a river in Queensland, he found a sizable egg, big-yolked like a bird's, encased in a leathery membrane like a lizard's and all ready for laying. He relayed his monumental discovery to the British Association for the Advancement of Science—then meeting in Montreal—in a classic four-word telegram: "Monotremes oviparous, ovum meroblastic," which confirmed that monotremes do lay eggs and described what kind.

THE day after Caldwell's discovery of the reproductive eccentricities of the platypus, another investigator, William Haacke, found eggs in another of the monotremes, little known then and little known even now, yet no less bizarre and considerably more widespread and numerous than the platypus. This was one of the spiny anteaters, or "echidnas," fully dry-land animals whose range includes most of Australia, New Guinea and Tasmania as well. The Australian spiny anteaters all belong to a short-nosed genus, *Tachyglossus*. The New Guinea ones include several larger, longer-nosed species of the genus *Zaglossus*. One of the first records of a spiny anteater may be found inscribed in the log of H.M.S. *Providence* under the command of Captain William Bligh, of H.M.S. *Bounty* fame. In an entry dated February 7, 1792, Bligh described it as "seventeen inches long, and has a small flat head connected so close to the shoulders that it can scarce be said to have a neck. It has no mouth like any other animal, but a kind of duck bill, two inches long, which opens at the extremity and will not admit anything above the size of a pistol ball. It has four legs and on each foot are very sharp claws; it has no tail, but a rump not unlike a penguin's, on which are quills of rusty brown."

Superficially, the spiny anteater is nothing like the platypus. It has a rotund, well-nigh tail-less torso and shuffles across the dry land in rocky country or forest. It comes along with its own organic fortress of sharp quills, somewhat like a porcupine. When frightened, however, it does dig—so proficiently that in soft soil it can literally vanish into the ground before the startled onlooker. It goes down all over at once, all in the same spot, with all four limbs scrabbling prodigiously together. It is probably aided in this feat by its peculiar hind paws, which are so splayed that the claws actually point to the rear rather than forward. When surprised on a rocky surface where digging or running is of no avail, it wedges its small body in among the stones and holds fast with the tenacity of a barnacle. So strong is it that one specimen kept in a zoologist's kitchen overnight succeeded in moving all the heavy furniture but the cookstove, which was anchored by a pipe, out toward the middle of the room in order to take an uninterrupted reconnaissance of its prison walls.

Like the platypus, the anteater subsists on a highly specialized diet of invertebrates which it takes in through a small mouth at the end of a long leathery snout. Instead of prawns and mussels, however, the food consists almost entirely of ants and termites. It rips its way into the nests of these insects with powerful foreclaws and picks off the inhabitants with a long, sticky protractile tongue. In its hunting equipment, it exactly parallels the totally unrelated, and in other respects totally different, placental anteaters of South America.

Beneath the two very different masks which the monotremes have donned along their separate paths to success, there are many fundamental likenesses which establish their identity as a group and their level of evolution. A primitive generalized reptile of the type from which all mammals are thought to have been derived differs from a placental mammal in countless details of structure, some of which the monotremes have retained. Thus, the reptile has a comparatively heavy and inelegant skeleton, including a number of bones which have been reduced or entirely done away with in mammals. The monotremes, however, still show reptilian features of bone structure in their hip and shoulder regions. Their legs are stubby like those of the early reptiles but, instead of sprawling out to the side, they are drawn in more under the body. Two large bones in the hinge of the reptilian jaw have shrunk marvelously in mammals and moved back into the head to become the tiny "hammer" and "anvil" bones which transmit vibrations to the inner ear. This transformation is complete in monotremes but the ears still remain somewhat reptilian in that they lack external pinnae, or sound-catching apparatus, on the head.

Teeth, which are normally important clues in classifying animals, are of no help where monotremes are concerned because as adults they have none. The platypus starts life with a set of brittle, irregular, toothlike structures which are shortly replaced by horny plates. The spiny anteaters, if their ancestors ever had teeth, have lost all trace of them.

In the vital matter of brain, all the monotremes, and particularly the spiny anteaters, are far better endowed than reptiles. Indeed, they have as much cerebral cortex as the lowliest marsupials or placentals. Both they and the marsupials, however, lack a bundle of nerve fibers, called the *corpus callosum*, which interconnects the two halves of the cortex, apparently serving as a communication channel between the left and right halves of the brain.

The senses which serve the monotremes include keen hearing and fair eyesight. The bill of a platypus is a mass of nerves relaying tactile sensations. The anteater snout is backed by ganglia which argue an acute sense of smell. Unlike most higher mammals, none of the monotremes have whiskers with which to feel their way in the dark. When burrowing, the platypus is said to have a mysterious awareness of cavities in the earth ahead, which enables it to avoid breaking through into adjacent rabbit warrens, rat holes or other platypus tunnels. The platypus makes no communicative sound except a tiny growl. As for the spiny anteaters, they are not known to break silence at all, except for a small snuffling sound which they sometimes make while drinking.

A principal difference between reptiles and mammals concerns their body temperature control. "Cold-blooded" reptiles rely heavily on sunshine to warm their blood, to keep their metabolic processes percolating and their nerves and muscles active. This subservience to the temperature of the surrounding air

THREE KINDS OF BIRTH

Among mammals there are three structural plans for reproduction, illustrated here by three anteaters: a monotreme, a marsupial and a placental. Although all three have developed similar adaptations of tongue and claw, their reproductive tracts (in color) are basically dissimilar. The primitive monotreme has a common excretory and egg-laying opening, the cloaca. The marsupial plan allows an embryo to grow in a small uterus, from which it passes at birth through a single external opening. The placental system is more advanced; the reproductive and excretory ducts are completely separated.

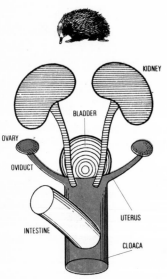

KIDNEY

BLADDER

OVARY

OVIDUCT

INTESTINE

UTERUS

CLOACA

SPINY ANTEATER: MONOTREME

The monotreme egg is formed in the ovary, then passes rather slowly through the oviduct, its leathery shell being formed along the way. By the time the shell is complete, the egg reaches the uterus and is quickly born via the animal's cloaca.

has been greatly lessened in the monotremes. The single ventricle of the primitive reptilian heart has been split into two chambers which keep separate the circulation to and from the lungs and vastly augment the supply of oxygen for the body's heat-producing chemical reactions. The intake of air has also been improved—by a diaphragm to help the lungs in inhaling and exhaling. The skin has been insulated in a warm coat of fur.

Through these major structural advances, which they share with marsupials and placentals, the monotremes can maintain a high body temperature in all weathers except extreme cold. Their warm-bloodedness, however, does not quite match that of higher mammals. Their temperature averages 88° F., eight to nine degrees below that of most marsupials or placentals. Moreover, it fluctuates from a torpid 72° to an animated 96°. Two further refinements of heat regulation—shivering and sweating—have never been developed by the monotremes. However, marsupials sweat little, if at all, and even placentals cannot usually sweat all over, but only from a few restricted areas.

Having remained egg layers, the monotremes have held to a reptilian pattern in their reproductive organs. The tubes down which the eggs pass from the ovaries of the female do not join to form a womb as they do in placental mammals, but remain separate until they empty into the urinary tract. This in turn discharges almost at once into the lowest stretch of the intestine, a short, stout pipe known as the cloaca. The same single terminal tube also serves in the male to convey the sperm. During mating, the lowermost portion of the male's cloaca protrudes somewhat and is reportedly used as an organ of insemination. It is because the platypus and spiny anteaters fulfill all their body processes through this one exit of the cloaca that they are classified as "monotremes"—from the Greek *mono*, meaning one, and *trema*, meaning hole.

To take the place of the cloaca, the placental mammals have developed separate outlets for the digestive, reproductive and urinary tracts. Marsupials, like monotremes, have only one, a much reduced cloaca—but the principal difference lies in the internal arrangement of the three systems.

In the placental female, each of the oviducts leads into a structure called the womb, or uterus, where the fertilized egg forms vascular connections with the maternal circulation through which the developing embryo is fed. In most of the Australian marsupials the oviducts come together and generally form a single chamber where the embryo undergoes a short period of development. However, the vagina itself is divided in two. Instead of proceeding down one or the other of these so-called lateral vaginas, the embryo housed in the now elongated uterus breaks out into the cloaca through which the young are born. This improvised birth canal, which the embryo tears open, remains clear in some marsupial females after the first pregnancy. In other species it heals over and the scar tissues are broken again with each delivery.

Depending on species, the marsupial embryo remains in the mother's body for eight to 40 days, as compared with 16 to 630 days for placental mammal species. While in the pouch, it is nourished through a nipple to which it attaches itself so firmly that removal of the animal may cause it injury. At first it grows comparatively slowly, but as its days in the pouch become numbered, it develops all in a rush.

Compared to the complexities of marsupial or placental birth, monotreme reproduction takes place with primitive straightforwardness. The fertilized egg simply slides down the cloaca and is laid. On the way—in a faint foreshadow-

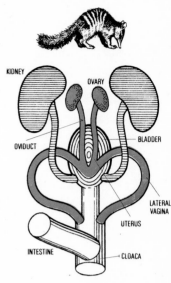

BANDED ANTEATER: MARSUPIAL

After the marsupial egg has been fertilized by sperm passing through a lateral vagina, it grows in the central uterus. The embryo then breaks through the uterine wall and passes through the cloaca. Afterward the temporary break heals over.

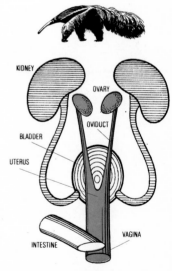

GREAT ANTEATER: PLACENTAL

Placental development takes place in a central uterus, which expands markedly to accommodate the embryo as it grows. This allows it to attain greater development before birth, which takes place through a separate opening, the vagina.

ing of placental developments—it may derive from its mother a certain amount of nourishment which diffuses through the rubbery shell of the egg.

For the reception of her eggs, a female platypus builds a nest of leaves, tucked away in a special breeding tunnel which she excavates in the banks of her home river or lake. Here the mother platypus normally lays two eggs in succession which become cemented together by their sticky casings when she curls up around them to keep them warm. During the seven to 14 days that it takes for them to hatch, she eats nothing and never leaves the burrow, except perhaps at the very end of her vigil when she may go out for a hurried swim and a quick grooming of her coat. Finally, the infant platypuses, hardly more than half an inch long, cut their way out of their adjoining shells by means of sharp projections on the tops of their bills. These so-called egg teeth, common enough among baby reptiles and birds, but unknown elsewhere in the mammal world, drop off shortly after birth.

For the first few days, the tiny blind platypuses get no food. The mother periodically leaves them while she takes a dip in the stream to forage for food for herself. Eventually her milk begins to break out like sweat from the pores on her abdomen and the little ones lap it off avidly. What starts the lactation has not yet been established. David Fleay once saw a platypus mother scratching her belly as though to stimulate milk flow; the late Harry Burrell, a pioneering platypus expert, believed that this function was performed by the young themselves by means of the caruncle, a soft, fleshy knob on their bills.

During nursing, the mother hunts mightily for food and sometimes eats almost as much as her own body weight in a day. After 17 weeks, when they are just over a foot long, the young begin to venture forth with her and learn the rudiments of swimming and hunting. In captivity, the mother has been observed to stay with them a month or two longer, playing with them, nuzzling them, growling at them and swimming circles around them.

The habits of the platypus are well known because the creature makes a charming, though delicate pet. By comparison, the spiny anteater is a prickly personality at best. It smells strongly of formic acid from the ants it eats. And, though it combs out its quills meticulously with the long index claw on each of its queer hind feet—claws thought to be especially developed for this purpose —it still achieves nothing of the cleanliness of the water-loving duckbill.

Insofar as is known, the female anteater lays her egg—or eggs—and cares for them with about the same amount of solicitude as the platypus. Being a

THE HOME OF THE PLATYPUS

The platypus burrow is a winding tunnel dug in a river bank by the female. The nesting chamber at the end has a lining of moist Eucalyptus leaves and grasses which keeps the newly laid eggs from drying and shriveling. Along the main passageway are false turns from which soil is mined to plug the burrow at various points, either for security or to maintain humidity. Occasionally the same underground home is enlarged and renovated year after year, and the resulting maze may be up to 100 feet long. The entrance, often beneath a fringe of roots, is close to the water, since platypuses gather their food on the river bottom. At the far right, a male courts a female, grabbing her by the tail while the pair swims in circles. The male keeps a separate burrow the year round; in fact platypuses are usually solitary animals.

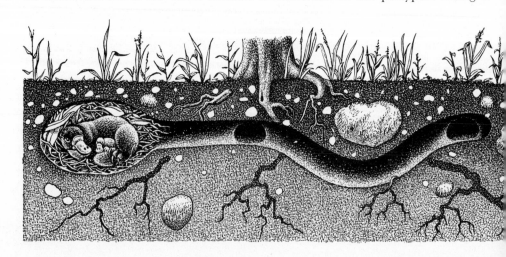

wandering animal, however, without permanent abode, she carries her eggs about with her after they are laid. For this purpose, during the breeding season she develops a special pouch which covers the area of milk pores on her underside. Here the eggs hatch and the young lap up sustenance during their first weeks of life. Eventually, when the small anteaters become too spiny to carry any longer, the mother deposits them under bushes and in other hiding places while she goes foraging. She comes back when she can to suckle them until they are ready to fend for themselves.

The brood pouch of the female spiny anteater has been compared to the pouch of marsupial mothers and has been used as an argument to show that marsupials evolved from monotremes or that monotremes degenerated from marsupials. Research has shown, however, that the spiny anteater's pouch develops quite differently and disappears when no longer needed.

Unhappily, no fossils have yet been found in any continent which reveal the lineage of the monotremes prior to the last few million years in Australia itself. Following the lead of the eminent evolutionary authority George Gaylord Simpson, however, zoologists generally agree that the monotremes' ancestors must have branched from the premammal stock and reached Australia at least 135 million years ago, perhaps even as long as 200 million years ago.

In those distant times, fossils show that the earth crawled with a variety of premammals. These premammals had begun as a ripple on the tide of reptilian life in the Pennsylvanian, about 280 million years ago. The first of them, called synapsids, left bones and teeth which departed increasingly, as the ages passed, from ordinary reptilian structure. From roughly 280 to 180 million years ago, mammal-like reptiles, branching from the synapsid stock, spread through Africa, western Europe and North America and gave rise to scores of kinds of beasts, some as bulky as alligators or donkeys, some as diminutive as mice or geckos.

SINCE we have only bones and teeth to go on, we do not know whether any of these premammals were clad in fur, whether they laid eggs or whether they gave milk. We know only that during the early Jurassic period, 180 to 166 million years ago, they were replaced by descendants which are classified, on the basis of skull and jaw structure, as the earliest true mammals. At first, if we disregard the mysterious living monotremes, there were at least four separate groups of pioneer mammals. These were gradually thinned out until, by about 60 million years ago, only the descendants of one group were left: the marsupials and the placentals.

Did the premammals—the mammal-like reptiles—all become extinct during the Jurassic, or are the Australasian monotremes their living survivors? The answer to this question depends on definitions and semantics: on where to draw the line between reptiles and mammals and on how to interpret the word "survivors" when marsupials and placentals also "survive"—survive, moreover, from what must be, far enough back, the same ancestral stock.

Many zoologists believe that since premammal days the monotremes have evolved far less than other living mammals in their basic reproductive and skeletal structure. For untold eons evolution has changed them mainly by perfecting their adaptations to their ant-eating and aquatic specializations. This, surely, is most remarkable. Why, having once begun to enjoy the advantages of large brains and maternal care, were the monotremes not pushed on through the ages by the same forces of selection and survival that shaped the other mammals? Perhaps the collective genetic potential of their race was simply not rich enough—did not supply enough variations and combinations for evolution to work upon. But what kept the monotreme heredity in this impoverished condition? What prevented a wealth of new genes and combinations of genes from accumulating over the course of generations?

This is one of the recurrent riddles of evolution and as yet there is no answer to it except the tree of life itself. The main stem of the tree appears always to have been pushed upward from one level to the next by small unspecialized animals that compete at many ways of life; creatures of such flexibility that they can sometimes find survival value in gene changes affecting their basic anatomy. Looking back, we see how periodically the main stem of evolution branches out in a great cluster of limbs and twigs which biologists call a radiation. At the twig-ends, the animals usually occupy highly specialized and demanding niches which discourage fundamental changes in anatomy. As a consequence, the specialists of one radiation may be replaced by those of a later, more advanced radiation which successfully competes for the same niche. Sometimes, however, they are not replaced. Sometimes they may simply specialize so well for their niches that they go on surviving in them through radiation after radiation.

In all likelihood the monotremes fit into this broad picture of life as the living twig-ends of an early mammalian radiation which took place in the world more than 135 million years ago. They have survived because they have specialized marvelously and entrenched themselves deeply in the niches they occupy. According to George Gaylord Simpson, the platypus and spiny anteater families are "markedly divergent . . . and must have been separated for a very long time." He goes on to suggest that animals "near the arbitrary reptile-mammal line . . ." probably "reached Australia in the . . . Triassic or in the Jurassic, that they there gave rise to the monotremes of stricter definition, and that the latter have . . . always been confined to the Australian region. It is completely speculative," he writes, "but is an interesting speculation, that there may have been a . . . monotreme radiation in Australia that was mostly, yet not entirely, replaced by a later . . . marsupial radiation."

Short of an adequate fossil find in the future, we shall never know what this possible Australian radiation of egg layers encompassed. Platypus and spiny anteater, through their anatomies, speak in generalities about their forebears but not in specifics about their extinct presumed cousins. Some idea, however, of the variations which may be played on a single evolutionary theme can be gleaned from the astonishing radiation of the marsupials described hereinafter.

EQUIPPED TO LIVE IN TWO WORLDS, THE PLATYPUS ALWAYS EATS ITS MEALS WHILE FLOATING, WITH EYES AND NOSTRILS ABOVE WATER

The Monotremes

Isolated in the Australasian region for millions of years, the only living monotremes—the platypus and the spiny anteaters—go their separate ways, having little in common except their primitive ancestry. The aquatic platypus is rare today, but the adaptable anteater is surprisingly common. Protected by its sharp spines, it has invaded nearly every land habitat but open desert.

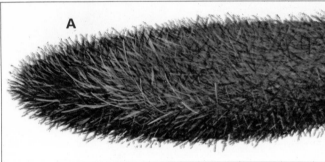

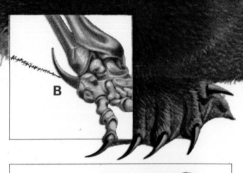

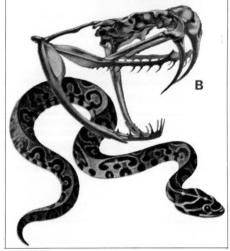

The Puzzling Platypus

Scientists of 150 years ago refused to believe in the platypus. It seemed to be a composite creature—part reptile, part mammal and part bird. Actually the platypus is unique; on a primitive body is superimposed a diversity of tools for locomotion, defense and feeding. Its flat, muscular tail (A), like the beaver's, acts as a stabilizer when it swims and assists in quick

dives. But it is covered with fur instead of scales. The curved poison spur (B) on the male's hind leg is similar to a pit viper's fangs. Like the viper's, it is hollow but carries a less deadly venom. Its webbed forefoot (C) is like the otter's, except that its skin extends beyond the toes to make an extra-large paddle. It depends on these paddles for swimming, whereas the otter

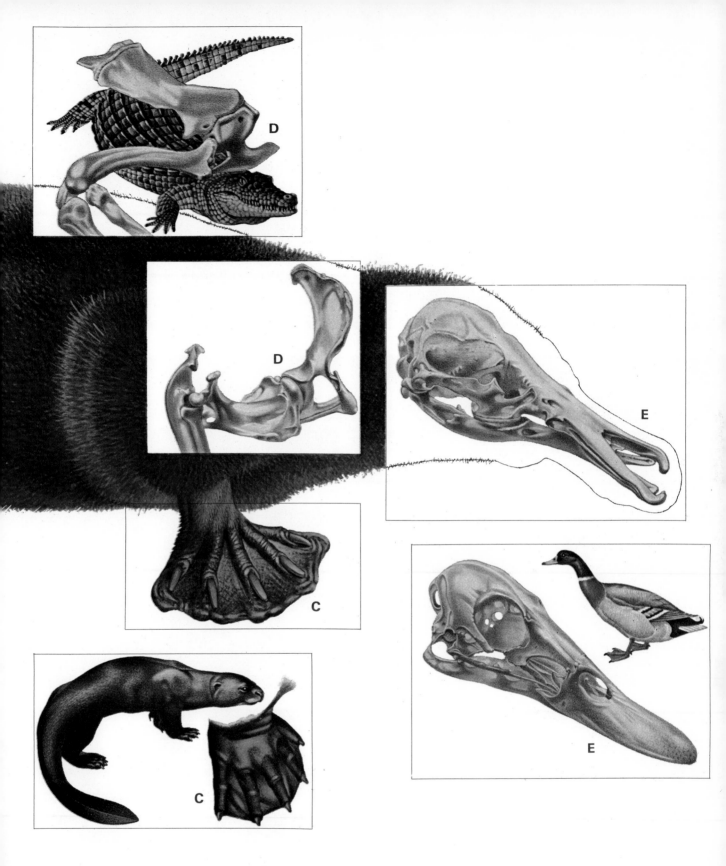

swims chiefly by undulations of its body. On land, the platypus' excess webbing folds under so that the strong claws can dig unimpaired. Its shoulder girdle (D) is a reminder of a remote reptilian past. Because of this clumsy connection of the forelimbs, the platypus shuffles close to the ground, but its stance is less sprawling than a crocodile's. Finally, the platypus and the duck both forage on mud bottoms—which accounts for the evolution of bills of similar shape. The comparison, however, goes only skin deep in the mammal, which has a strikingly different pronged structure (E) supporting a bill that is actually a moist, nerve-filled organ, flexible and sensitive to vibrations or touch, unlike a bird's hard, horny bill.

EYES AND EARS CLOSED BY A SINGLE FOLD OF SKIN, THE PLATYPUS DIVES FOR FOOD. IT USES ONLY ITS WEBBED FOREFEET IN SWIMMING

IN A MINUTE, THE SENSITIVE BILL LOCATES WORMS (ABOVE), WHICH ARE STORED IN CHEEK POUCHES AS IT PREPARES TO SURFACE (BELOW)

ARRIVING AT NEW YORK'S BRONX ZOO IN JUNE, 1958, A FIVE-MONTH-OLD FEMALE RESTS JUST AS SHE WOULD IN THE BURROW—ON HER TAIL

A Fresh-Water Bottom Feeder

Access to fresh water is vital to the existence of the platypus, which, in the breeding season, may need as much as three miles of stream or lake shore as its exclusive domain. Despite its dependence on water, the platypus spends only about two hours a day in it, foraging efficiently along the mud bottom during active feeding periods at dawn and again at dusk.

Platypuses have apparently been well adapted to a riverine life for more than a million years. It is only in the last hundred years that their existence has been threatened. In the latter part of the 19th

Century they were extensively trapped for their very soft, molelike fur. In addition, many were accidentally caught and drowned in fish traps. As a result, they became so rare in the coastal rivers that the Australian government placed the species under strict protection. Now some populations are increasing, according to a census taken in New South Wales in 1954. Only seven live platypuses have ever been displayed outside of the country—all in the Bronx Zoo. The last of these died in 1959 and it seems unlikely that any will be exported again.

A Mystery of Birth

Although spiny anteaters are common in Australia, almost nothing is known about their breeding habits. Like the platypus, the anteater is an egg layer, but it does not dig a nesting burrow. Instead, the mother develops a temporary pouch of skin, drawn together by muscular contractions, where the single egg is probably incubated and the baby stays until almost full grown. Does the pouch form before the egg is laid? If so, how is the egg transferred from the egg-laying duct? Since no one has ever seen a "delivery," the answers to these questions are entirely speculative. The drawing at right is a guess at the "birth" position and the placement of the egg.

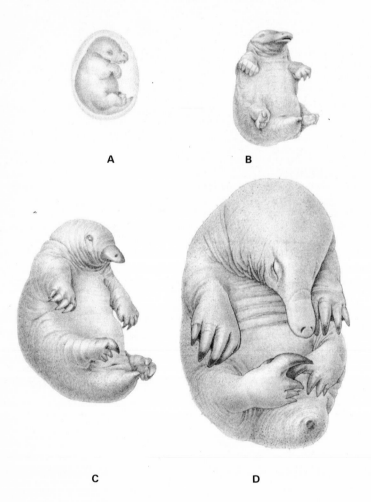

A   B

C   D

FROM EGG TO EJECTION FROM THE POUCH, four stages in the development of the spiny anteater are shown above left. The embryo in the egg (A), about two weeks old, is ready for hatching. A mere half inch long, it has an egg tooth on the snout similar to a reptile's or a bird's, used to break through the shell. This tool has dropped off at about three and a half weeks (B). The feet and claws are well-defined when the baby reaches the probable age of five weeks (C). Spines sprout at about nine weeks (D) and will soon be prominent and painful enough to annoy the mother. At about 10 weeks she forces the prickly bundle out of the pouch and hides it in a bush, a hollow log or small burrow. She may then return periodically

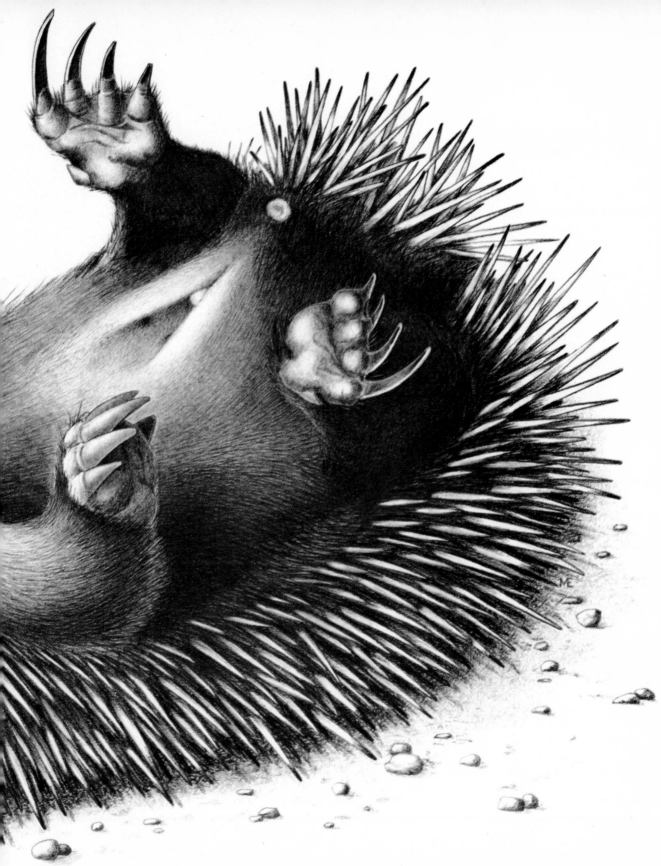

to allow her offspring to nurse until it is more fully developed. The pouch, shown in the drawing above right, opens toward the stomach and encloses the pores through which milk flows and is lapped from the skin and fur by the young. Tests under anesthesia show that when the abdominal muscles relax, this shallow pocket disappears in seconds. Normally, the animal has a pouch only in the breeding season. What stimulates its formation—and when—is still a mystery, as is the means by which the egg gets into the pouch. The most logical view is that it drops into place upon being laid—with the animal's body curled to receive it, although the possibility also exists that it is maneuvered into position by the snout or forelegs.

The Defensive Anteaters

Of primary importance to the spiny anteater is the way its quills combine with a powerful digging ability to help it survive. For a small unaggressive animal with a twiglike nose, no teeth and a soft underbelly, what could be better than the ability to sink right out of sight into the ground—either to avoid being seen or to guard against being flipped over by some dexterous predatory paw—and at the same time ensure that, during the few critical seconds spent digging, there will be a thick hedge of short but extremely sharp spines to protect the digger's back.

The Australian spiny anteater, shown here, is normally smaller than its New Guinea cousins, whose spines lie concealed in thick fur needed to withstand the cold of altitudes up to 8,000 feet. The New Guinea species have long, curved snouts for probing layers of wet humus in the cloud forest.

WITH QUILLS RAISED for protection while digging, a trio of anteaters starts to submerge in loose soil on Donna Buang Mountain in Victoria. The dark youngster in the foreground is almost spineless.

OUT OF SIGHT in a matter of seconds, the spiny anteater shown in the four pictures at right works all feet simultaneously. It pushes earth out to the sides and sinks straight down into the ground.

4

The Meat Eaters: from Mice to Devils

THE ancestors of the platypus and spiny anteaters, as nearly as we can tell, had the mammal role in Australia pretty much to themselves for most of the 70-million-year span of the Cretaceous period. Then, about 70 million years ago, there is believed to have come to that ancient land a new kind of animal, the marsupial. Being more efficient and more highly evolved than egg-laying mammals, it gradually infiltrated every province and crevice of the country, until none were left of the monotremes which may have preceded it except the stream dwellers and the predators of ants.

In the course of their radiation, the marsupials came to ply almost every sort of animal trade known to mammals elsewhere—from treetop leaf-eating to grassland grazing, from snapping up small insects to killing sizable birds and lizards. In some of the more specialized of these roles, the marsupials gradually acquired habits and appearances similar to those that their placental counterparts were developing in other parts of the world. Among zoologists such a tendency of totally unrelated creatures to develop similar body forms and habits is called convergence, and no fauna anywhere today provides more illustrations of it than do the Australian marsupials. Some of them look startlingly like mice, wolves, moles or cats. Still others look vaguely like rabbits or squirrels. And then again a great many more—the kangaroos, for instance—look like nothing else on earth.

There are 108 different species of pouched animals found in Australia, plus 67 more that have various distributions in Australia, New Guinea and other nearby islands. In the final analysis the members of this varied menagerie are most intriguing not because of their resemblances to familiar beasts, but because of their strangeness. In giving them names, the early Australian settlers responded to this strangeness with a fine sense of outback poetry, distinguishing wombat from numbat, cuscus from sugar glider, wallaroo from nail-tail, wallaby from pademelon, mulgara from tuan, bandicoot from bilby, devil from thylacine—and, of course, koala from kangaroo.

In approaching this rich confusion of exotic names and animals, zoologists began by opening the mouth of their problem and looking at teeth. Australasian marsupials have two basic kinds of dentition: the so-called polyprotodont marsupials have many small, sharp front teeth and are largely meat eaters. The diprotodont marsupials have a pair of specialized incisors standing out from the other teeth in the front of their lower jaws and are mainly herbivores. For the most part the meat eaters have retained a primitive five-digit condition in their feet and forepaws, while most of the plant eaters have developed a fusion of the second and third toes on each hind foot. The bandicoots, with feet like the plant eaters and teeth like the meat eaters, have the feeding habits of both.

The intermediate bandicoots, in the classification scheme of zoology, are usually considered a single family. The plant eaters are normally split into five families: the kangaroos and wallabies; the rat kangaroo; the wombats; and two families of treetop dwellers that include phalangers, gliding possums and the koala. The carnivores number four families: the small marsupial "mice"; the somewhat larger "cats" and "devils"; the still larger Tasmanian "wolf"; two kinds of marsupial moles; and finally the marsupial anteaters, or numbats.

Because of their five-toed hind feet and simple front teeth, the marsupial beasts of prey are thought to be the most primitive of the Australasian pouched animals. They come closest to resembling the living polyprotodont opossums of the New World and various fossils of opossumlike creatures which have been found in both North America and Europe. The best present-day scientific speculation indicates that the first marsupials—with teeth and bones similar to those of American opossums and not much different from those of the smallest Australian meat eaters—appeared in North America about 80 million years ago and did not show up in Europe until a good many million years later. In these two temperate outposts they became extinct at least 25 million years ago. In Australasia and South America they went on to survive up to the present. The common American opossum has survived so well that when the Panamanian land bridge arose out of the ocean more than two million years ago, it escaped the extermination which overtook many of its fellows, spread north into Central America and is still spreading north in the United States today.

Australian fossil beds have hardly been tapped as yet, but marsupial remains have been recovered that go back about 25 million years. These show that the more advanced marsupials, the plant eaters, had by then already split off from meat-eater stock. Taken all together, these fragments of evidence suggest that the first Australian marsupials were offshoots of opossumlike or mouselike predators which spread widely through the world in the Cretaceous and perhaps

seizes its victims by the nape of the neck, kills them, skins them and then, after daintily grooming itself, eats them. In lazier moments, it is sometimes seen basking like a lizard in the noonday sun, unlike many other marsupial "mice," which are nocturnal.

The beautiful tuan, or brush-tailed *Phascogale*, runs as large as a wharf rat, and to treat it as a marsupial mouse could cost a man a finger. During the days of the great mice plagues in the early part of this century, it used to lurk on the edges of the rodent hordes, picking off stragglers. The tuan is a rare animal today, but to early settlers it was a nuisance, a bloodthirsty poultry killer, and had a reputation for being a kleptomaniac of odds and ends that struck its fancy as nest furnishings. Story has it that two lumbermen logging alone together in a camp outback once came to near blows because of a pound note that had vanished. Later, after felling a tree, they found the note in it, neatly built into a tuan's nest.

Whereas *A. flavipes* and some of the other broad-foots have ridged pads on their paws, which enable them to climb on rough rock and bark, the narrow-foots mostly hunt on unridged feet, seldom climb and generally inhabit open country, even deserts. Their pouches are generally better developed than those of the broad-foots. The more specialized and streamlined of them, the jerboa marsupials, travel in staccato hops, doing so much of their moving on their hind legs that they look like replicas in miniature of their remote relatives, the plant-munching kangaroos.

Jerboa marsupials get their name from their resemblance to true jerboas, desert-dwelling rodents from Africa and Asia. To complicate matters, the Australian desert contains its own separately evolved jerboa mice—not marsupials, but typical rodents with typical plant-gnawing rodent teeth in the front of their mouths. These two groups of small jumping animals, though they resemble each other uncannily, are—and it must be emphasized again—completely different. One consists of carnivorous marsupials, the other consists of plant-and-seed-eating rodents. More confusing still, they are said to occupy the same burrows, since the marsupial does not dig a hole of its own but prefers to move in with the more industrious rodent.

S ETTLEMENT of the country by humans, and more specifically the cutting of timber and clearing of brush, together with the introduction of such animals as dogs, cats and foxes, has tended to push the smaller marsupial carnivores farther and farther into the wilder sections of Australia. In spite of this, they are managing to hold their own remarkably well in the places where they still are found. Quite different is the story of the larger marsupial meat eaters —the pouched cats and wolves. The wolves are almost extinct. And the cats, though they still occasionally maraud hen roosts and are even found living among the rocks in suburbs of Sydney, are becoming increasingly rare.

The smallest of the marsupial cats is known as the northern native cat. It is a little larger than a good-sized rat and is elegantly spotted with white on its body, but not its tail. The tiger cat is spotted all over, including the tail, and runs as large as a domestic cat. It climbs easily, attacks with reckless abandon and hangs on with bulldog perseverance. Excited by blood, both have a tendency, like weasels, to kill beyond their needs. In a chicken coop they become so engrossed that they can sometimes be clubbed to death before they will give up their victims and make a break for it. They are less intelligent than placental wildcats, but their limbs and muscles are magnificent. The tiger cat has been

NONCONVERGENCE

Similar habits are no guarantee that two animals will develop along the same lines: the placental impala of Africa (above) and the marsupial kangaroo of Australia (below), although their jaws and teeth reveal that both are grazing animals, are otherwise astonishingly different. The impala has long and slender legs for running from predators, the kangaroo a pair of enormous hind legs for bounding away. In addition they defend themselves quite differently: the impala with its horns, the kangaroo by rearing up on its tail and disemboweling a foe with the claws of its hind feet.

known to kill a large placental tomcat in a fair fight and to hold dogs at bay. Such is its heedless daring that it is reputed to spring at a bird on a tree limb and fall with it through unplumbed depths of darkness to the ground.

On the mainland of Australia, the fate that may well be in store for these superb archaic feline beasts of prey has already overtaken two other distinctive marsupial hunters, the devil and the wolf. Fossils show that both formerly ranged the continent. In recent historic times, both have been restricted to Tasmania. The devil is still to be seen in the forest reserves and national parks of that southern island. The wolf is not seen at all, and has not been since about 1930. But several expeditions, sent out to look for it—the last in 1961 —claim to have found its footprints in dense rain forest along the Tasmanian west coast.

Both devil and wolf could have been hounded toward extinction by a true placental dog, the dingo, now well established as a wild species in Australia since its introduction by aboriginal man a good many thousand years ago. The devil is a heavy-set black beast, blotched with white, about three feet long, with short stumpy legs, an immense head and massive, bone-crunching jaws. Except when still a cub, it moves slowly, climbs poorly and altogether seems far better equipped for eating than catching. Be this as it may, it has survived far better than the wolf and has found many ways of getting along on its own. It does feast on carrion, because it can be caught with well-aged baits of flesh. But it also is reputed to be a killer of live poultry and even an occasional lamb. Away from the easy game of farm animals, it probably lies in wait for whatever it can catch, and it eats with a ravenous and undiscriminating appetite. Its heavy body, jaws and paws resemble those of a bear, and its tracks, found frequently along stream banks, suggest that it pampers a bearish tooth for crabs and crayfish, frogs and fish.

THE marsupial wolf, or thylacine, looks distinctly canine. Superficially it differs from a dog mainly in that it has an unpliant, unwagging, tapering tail and a set of dark zebra stripes on its back that look almost as if its ribs were showing through in the wrong places. It stands about three feet high at the shoulders and runs six feet in length. Its muzzle is long and "smiling," and its belly is tucked up tight under its ribs. Unlike other marsupials, it jogs along on its toes. It has canine fangs for grasping and piercing, well-developed molars for cutting and chewing flesh. But it is a marsupial. It has a small crescent-shaped pouch opening backward, enclosing teats enough for four young ones. Its brain, though relatively large, is typically marsupial. In running, it trots or breaks into a "shambling canter." It is not as fast as a dog, nor does it hunt in the canny complex social patterns of the pack. At most it runs in pairs and trails its quarry to earth more by perseverance than speed. Ten thousand years ago, with the possible exception of the now-extinct *Thylacoleo*, or marsupial cave lion, it was unquestionably the only Australian beast which the big kangaroos ever needed to avoid. More recently, an Australian, Hugh S. Mackay, wrote a description of its encounter with a placental dog, which serves as a fine elegy to its former prowess and imminent passing. "A bull-terrier," he wrote, "was once set upon a wolf and bailed it up in a niche in some rocks. There the wolf stood, with its back to the wall, turning its head from side to side, checking the terrier as it tried to butt in from alternate and opposite directions. Finally, the dog came in close, and the wolf gave one sharp, foxlike bite tearing a piece of the dog's skull clean off, and it fell with the brain protruding, dead."

A GREEDY HUNTER, THE BRUSH-TAILED PHASCOGALE, OR TUAN, ATTACKS PREY LARGER THAN ITSELF, OFTEN KILLING MORE THAN IT CAN EAT

Rodents False and True

When is a mouse not a mouse? None of the mouse-like creatures shown here really are—except the one in the photograph at right. The others, with the deceptiveness so typical of many of Australia's animals, blend the look of true herbivorous rodents with the meat-eating habits of placental shrews and weasels. Some, like the fat-tailed marsupial mouse at left, are ground dwellers that hunt for insects. Others, like the phascogale, have broad, corrugated foot pads which enable them to hunt rodents and birds in trees as well as on the ground.

The delicate mouse at right is a true rodent, a representative of a group of placental seed eaters that has been in Australia for several million years. Known as pseudo mice, these tiny rodents have only four teats, fewer than most familiar mice and rats. Preyed upon by marsupial mice, and subject to competition from larger native rats and introduced mice, they are still managing to hold their own.

THE DELICATE MOUSE, so named for its tiny size and subtle color, is a ground-dwelling placental that eats seeds. It is preyed upon by owls and snakes—and by marsupial mice.

THE FAT-TAILED MARSUPIAL MOUSE, APTLY NAMED, STORES UP CALORIES IN ITS TAIL TO WITHSTAND TIMES OF FAMINE

Two Cats and a Numbat

Larger than the marsupial mice, and much rarer, are two catlike carnivores, the native cat and the tiger cat. The latter is a solitary, partly arboreal animal with a reputation for being the most combative creature of the Australian bush. The native cat lives in hollow logs or rock piles. Its present scarcity is partly due to its lack of caution—or, to put it another way, its stupidity. Rabbit traps are a great hazard to it, and one source speaks of native cats that practically queued up for the privilege of getting caught. As a consequence, they are sometimes seen hobbling along on three legs, occasionally on only two.

The numbat is entirely different from these active hunters. It is a small, slow-moving, totally inoffensive anteater that prowls about on the forest floor looking for termites. Its conspicuous, beautifully banded body and leisurely ways make it an easy mark for cats, dogs and foxes, and today it is nearly extinct. An extremely gentle animal, it never struggles or bites when caught. If molested, it limits itself to uttering a few faint, protesting grunts.

A NATIVE CAT forages with five spotted young clinging to its back. It is said to bear up to 24 babies in a litter, but has only six teats, and as a result most of the babies perish. At maturity this animal reaches a length of a little over two feet.

THE NUMBAT, about the size of a gray squirrel, is strikingly marked with black-and-white bands. It has the elongated snout of an anteater, which makes room in its mouth for 52 teeth, more than are found in any other kind of marsupial.

THE TIGER CAT is somewhat larger but shorter-legged than the native cat. It has a spotted coat and a spotted tail. A good climber, it spends most of its time skulking in the forest, and although a ferocious fighter, is seldom seen by man.

The Wolf and the Devil

The largest marsupial carnivore remaining in the world is the Tasmanian wolf, a lanky, dog-shaped animal with stripes on its back and a tapering tail. A shy, nocturnal hunter, it is not particularly swift, but catches its prey by sheer persistence, dogging it to the point of exhaustion and then closing in for the kill. Unlike some other predators, it seldom makes more than a single meal of its victim, abandoning the leftovers to scavengers—among them the smaller, chunkier Tasmanian devil.

The devil's regular fare is rat kangaroos, lizards, frogs and birds, but it occasionally pulls down a small wallaby, relying on its cunning and great strength. Despite its name, it is an amiable animal if captured young, and makes a successful pet. Although rare today, it is in no immediate danger of extermination, since a good many individuals are protected in game preserves in Tasmanian forests.

THE LAST WILD SPECIMEN of a Tasmanian wolf ever shot was this one killed in 1930. Since then no confirmed sighting of a wild wolf has been made, though its footprints are reported.

THE LAST CAPTIVE wolf was photographed in 1933, caught in a yawn that revealed the wide, more-than-90-degree gape of its jaw. Also clearly shown are its oddly proportioned hind legs and its long, thick, drooping tail. Efforts to raise this rare carnivore in captivity have been unsuccessful. Invariably the animal has sulked and refused to eat, weakened and died.

SHORT-MUZZLED AND STOCKY, A TASMANIAN DEVIL GLARES FROM ITS LEAFY HIDEOU

5

The Mixed Feeders: Bilbies to Wallaroos

I F all the living things on earth were sorted out into piles according to the source of food on which they live, overwhelmingly the largest pile would turn out to be plants, most of which subsist on sunlight. Next in mass would rank the animals that eat the plants. And last would come the animals that prey on the plant eaters.

To this general rule Australasia is no exception. Not only are there many more plant-eating marsupials than there are flesh-eating ones, but many more individual kinds as well. As we have seen in the previous chapters, the carnivorous marsupials—the so-called cats, devils, wolves and mice—total no more than 52 species. The herbivorous kangaroos, on the other hand, come in a bewildering assortment numbered at about 45 species. And the kangaroos are only one of the three marsupial groups which contain plant eaters. The others are the tree-climbing phalangers (some 37 species) and the tailless terrestrial wombats (four species). The small, earth-scratching bandicoots (at least 19 species) are an intermediate group of mixed feeders which are sometimes lumped for discussion purposes with the plant eaters, although they feed largely on the immature forms of insects.

The diversity of the Australian herbivores, like that of plant-eating animals anywhere, is simply a result of the many opportunities afforded by vegetation. There are nectars to sip, seeds to crack, fruits to bite into, saps to tap, barks to strip, roots to dig and, most important, grasses to chew. From one kind of plant to another, these potential harvests vary in shape, accessibility, oiliness, dryness, toughness and innumerable other properties, not the least of which is digestibility. Since there is such a great variety of things to choose from, no herbivore can be expected to eat all parts of all plants, but only some parts of some plants. This they do by means of specialized claws, digits, paws and limbs with which to gather in their harvest, specialized teeth with which to chew and a specialized digestive tract with which to absorb what they have eaten.

Compared with plant food, animal food is relatively scarce and unvaried. The cat that eats mice may also eat birds, lizards and fish. The claws, cunning and digestive equipment that suffice for one kind of prey usually suffice for many others as well. As a result, the evolutionary pressures on carnivores have always been slightly different from the ones acting on herbivores. On every continent the meat eaters have developed improved senses, agility of foot, good meat-eating dentition and mobile habits. But in some other respects they have tended to remain more primitive and unspecialized than the plant eaters, and they have never split up into as many species. In their quest for game they have wider ranges, are less subject to geographical isolation, and stand always one step further removed from the land and vegetation around them.

Having invaded virtually every niche afforded by the various rainfall, temperature and vegetation zones of Australasia, the herbivorous marsupials are mirrors of their various environments. The phalangers are all treetop animals and so live mainly in forests. Some of them are exclusively tropical forms, inhabiting the rain forests of Queensland, New Guinea and the islands east of the Wallace Line. Others are temperate creatures restricted to the woodlands on the eastern and southwestern mainland coasts. A few range over both areas.

In contrast to the phalangers, the wombats are strictly ground dwellers—heavy-set, short-legged, tailless creatures, about three feet long. They walk stolidly on all four feet and dig burrows as much as 100 feet long for themselves. The kangaroos on the other hand, those bounciest of all marsupial families, have made a place for themselves in almost every kind of vegetation and habitat Australasia has to offer. They range from the deserts, where they browse on *Triodia* grass and saltbush, through savanna grassland and woodland to the tropical rain forests of New Guinea, northeastern Queensland, and the adjacent Aru, Salawati and Trobriand Islands. In the heartland of their empire, the savanna grassland and woodland belts, they have been greatly reduced by the activities of man, but elsewhere, as in the unsettled north and the interior, they survive in numbers and, in some cases, under conditions that are little short of astonishing. Some of the species of the arid regions, for example, appear to get along with almost no water at all: a recent campaign to rid certain marginal pasturelands of mountain kangaroos, or wallaroos, by poisoning their water holes ended in failure when the animals proved capable of giving up drinking entirely—surviving, apparently, on plant juices and the dew from leaves.

In their hopping gait, the kangaroos exhibit a characteristic of several mammals of grasslands and arid regions the world around. A saltatory, or jumping, mode of locomotion typifies the kangaroo rats of the American Southwest, the jerboas of the Sahara and the Asian steppes, the springhares of the African veld.

DIFFERENT TOES
FOR DIFFERENT USES

Bandicoots are all alike in having two of the toes of their hind feet joined together; why, no one is quite sure. They differ markedly from each other in the number and arrangement of their other toes. Some of these variations are shown in the drawings of the front and rear feet (left and right, respectively) of three species, and reflect the different uses to which the bandicoot feet are put.

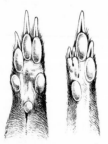

Unlike most other bandicoots, the short-nosed bandicoot is omnivorous, rather than insectivorous, and uses the sharp claws on its front feet to dig up grubs and bulbs. It defends itself by striking out and pummeling with all four feet.

And Australia, of course, in addition to large and small kangaroos, also has its jerboalike marsupials and small jerboalike rodents. The largest kangaroos appear merely to be gigantic embodiments of this worldwide arid land adaptation.

As to why hopping should be such a successful mode of locomotion in arid and open country, one can only guess. Perhaps an erratic pattern of movement —the ability to dodge and dart or make right-angle turns with confusing rapidity—affords the best protection to an animal living in an area with little vegetation to hide its activities from predators both on land and in the air.

S HARING the forests, grasslands and desert with the kangaroos are the bandicoots, a group of small to middle-sized animals distinguished by having many unspecialized front teeth like the marsupial carnivores and a fusion of second and third toes on their hind feet like the herbivores. These fused, or "syndactylous," toes, which also show up on the feet of climbing phalangers, trotting wombats and hopping kangaroos, are most interesting structures. Where they emerge from the foot, the second and third digits are bound together in a single sheath of skin and controlled muscularly as a unit. Out toward their tips, however, they separate into two toes, ending in a pair of distinct claws.

According to some students of marsupial mammals, the two-pronged fork at the tip of the syndactylous toe, when developed to its greatest extent, is used mainly as a comb for grooming the fur. Other mammalogists believe that this application is a secondary one and that the fork initially developed as an aid in climbing. This theory holds that a branch of early insect-eating marsupials with herbivorous tendencies acquired the double toe in specializing for treetop life. Some of them then took to the ground and became the bandicoots, while others stayed in the treetops to develop the teeth of phalangers. From these ancestral climbing creatures, with both diprotodont teeth and syndactylous toes, presumably descended not only the first phalangers, but also the later terrestrial wombats and kangaroos.

Because Australian gardeners were plagued by bandicoots digging up their flower beds, it was long assumed that they were plant eaters. Actually, while some may eat a certain amount of vegetable matter, they are primarily insectivorous and find a living by the curious habit of fossicking in leaf mold or loose soil. Instead of pouncing and biting, they scratch and scrabble. Instead of feeding on active adult insects, they prey mostly on sluggish grubs and larvae. They are really doing gardeners a service by digging out the root-ravening grubs of cockchafer beetles. When, as sometimes happens, a bandicoot turns more actively carnivorous and bandies blows with a rodent or even a fellow bandicoot, its ingrained feeding technique—all scratch and little bite—results in a display of belligerence and ferocity quite out of keeping with its appearance. During the early rounds of the battle, it hops back and forth over its antagonist, gashing out wounds in passing with its sharp hind claws. If it succeeds in weakening its foe by this hit-and-run tactic, it brings its forepaws into play and proceeds to scrabble its victim into the dust, constantly backing away and pawing the broken body toward it until nothing is left but a lifeless pulp.

Of the eight generally recognized genera of bandicoots, four are little-known tropical animals that potter about in the leaf litter of rain forests from northeastern Queensland across New Guinea to the island of Ceram. Two others inhabit a broad belt around the edge of the mainland, and the final two are found mainly in the interior. In size, they range from six inches to about two feet in length, of which roughly one third is tail. They have long sharp snouts,

Although only 18 inches long including its tail, the rabbit-eared bandicoot reputedly digs fast enough to keep ahead of a man with a shovel. It does its digging with the rather symmetrical front foot tipped with a single strong claw.

The pig-footed bandicoot gets its name from its "cloven" forefoot. Its hind foot has been modified until it has only one functional toe remaining, the others being mere appendages. It employs a running gait, whereas other bandicoots hop.

A TALE OF TAILS

A number of marsupials have prehensile tails that are well adapted for seizing and grasping. That of the ring-tailed possum (above) is so handy for holding tight that the possum can climb down trees headfirst, letting go with its forefeet and counting on the tight twist of its tail on a branch for safety.

More versatile, the tail of the brush-tailed rat kangaroo (below) is adapted for hauling. After looping it firmly around a bundle of grass, this tiny rat kangaroo hops off to its building site, trailing its neat parcel behind. Once it arrives, it will use its tail to shape and pack down the grass into a soft nest.

slight shoulders and stubby forelimbs, stout hindquarters and long rear feet. Their rather ratlike over-all appearance won them the name "bandicoot," which is a corruption of an Indian word "pandi-kokku," signifying "pig-rat."

In both looks and diet, the most distinctive of the bandicoots are the two genera which live in the arid regions of central Australia: the long-eared, rabbit-like bilbies (*Thylacomys*), which are said to eat mostly meat, and the small, graceful pig-feet (*Choeropus*), which are said to be purely vegetarian.

Whereas most bandicoots nest in shallow depressions scooped out of the ground and filled with camouflaging debris, the bilbies dig true burrows that spiral down as much as five feet into the earth. When trapped in these cul-de-sac warrens, they excavate impromptu escape hatches so fast that men with shovels can seldom keep pace with them. They sleep in the burrows during the day and ramble abroad after insects and mice at night. While sleeping they remain squatting, snout tucked between forepaws and ears wrapped around over eyes. From this strange snoozing stance, they sometimes come out only half-adjusted and lope off under the desert moon with one ear back and the other still drowsily draped forward.

While the bilby, except for its carnivorous inclinations, has developed resemblances to a rabbit, the vegetarian pig-footed bandicoot has tended in a swinelike direction. Each of its forepaws leaves a cloven print, stamped out by a single pair of functional fingers. Each of its hind feet is dominated by one large, weight-bearing toe that resembles a hoof. Its delicate limbs are reminiscent of those of deer or antelope, but its gait has been described as that of "a broken down hack in a canter."

Since it inhabits the most remote regions of the outback, the pig-foot has been seen alive by only a handful of explorers. For a long time it was known to science through a single faulty specimen. Bandicoots have an almost lizardlike way of losing their tails, and the first pig-foot ever collected happened to be without one. It was duly registered in a museum collection as *Ecaudatus*, the tailless. Two decades later, an enterprising Australian zoologist, finding himself in a camp of aborigines in the territory of the tailless pig-foot, drew pictures of the animal as best he could reconstruct it and offered a reward to any hunter who would catch him one. "The cunning natives," he wrote later, "not succeeding in finding the animal required, were in the habit of bringing any number of common bandicoot with the tail screwed out."

THE marsupials with syndactylous toes that took to the trees and became phalangers are a particularly fascinating family because they fill an arboreal world occupied in other lands by monkeys, sloths, opossums and squirrels. All too little is known about this mysterious overhead realm of life. In tropical and subtropical regions, it supports at least as many kinds of animals as the forest floor beneath it. What is more, it has evoked remarkably similar adaptations in altogether different groups of animals in different parts of the globe.

The Australasian treetops have become the home for at least 44 species of phalangers, which are grouped in 14 genera. Like monkeys, all phalangers have opposable big toes which enable them to use their hind paws as hands for grasping and holding. Many of them also have prehensile tails like the tree porcupines, spider monkeys, silky anteaters or opossums of South America. Another group of them has developed sailplane membranes with which to glide like the rodent flying squirrels and the so-called flying lemurs, or colugos.

Most of these amazingly specialized and distinct animals are known by

Australians as "possums"—not opossums or 'possums, but simply as possums without the apostrophe. The smallest of them frisk about like tree shrews and persist in the insect-eating habits presumed to have come from their ancestors. Several of the larger ones eat a mixed diet of leaves, fruits and insects, and look somewhat like kinkajous. The largest of all eat only leaves, which they gather in with the deliberate thoroughness of a sloth.

THE namegiver for this motley menagerie of acrobats is *Phalanger* itself, large possums up to four feet long, tail included, and more commonly known as cuscuses. Playing a role like that of the placental tree sloth in the rain forests of South America, the cuscus ranges more widely than any other marsupial through the tropical islands east and west of New Guinea. On the east it reaches into the Solomons and Admiralties, and on the west into Timor, Flores and Celebes. Because of its distribution, it helped Wallace to chart the boundary between Asia and Australasia, and one of the best descriptions of it extant was given by him in 1869.

"The curious genus *Cuscus* . . .," he wrote, "are opossum-like animals, with a long prehensile tail, of which the terminal half is generally bare. They have small heads, large eyes, and a dense covering of woolly fur, which is often pure white with irregular black spots or blotches, or sometimes ashy brown with or without white spots. They live in trees, feeding upon the leaves, of which they devour large quantities. They move about slowly, and are difficult to kill, owing to the thickness of their fur, and their tenacity of life. A heavy charge of shot will often lodge in the skin and do them no harm, and even breaking the spine or piercing the brain will not kill them for some hours. The natives everywhere eat their flesh, and as their motions are so slow, easily catch them by climbing; so that it is wonderful they have not been exterminated."

Of middle-sized possums smaller than the cuscus, the commonest are the brushtails of Australia and the ringtails of Australia and New Guinea. The two-foot-long ringtails are so named because they carry their prehensile tails curled downward in rings or question marks behind them. They eat leaves, fruits and blossoms, including those of introduced garden and orchard plants. One small group of them in the northwest has adapted to life in rock piles, but most are creatures of high forest or thick scrub. In the countryside near Sydney in southeastern Australia, the local ringtails often set up housekeeping in dense clumps of saplings or mistletoe, where they build dome-shaped nests the size of footballs out of leaves, twigs and bark.

The brawny brushtails, measuring up to three feet long, are still more common than the ringtails and have been described by one of Australia's leading mammalogists, Ellis Troughton, as "the only marsupials successfully adapting themselves to the changed conditions brought about by human 'enterprise.'" Why this should be so is a fascinating question. Here is an animal of stout body, sturdy claws, pert ears and foxy face which appears to be no more smart or spry or fast-breeding than many other marsupials. Moreover, its fine, long fur and bushy tail—sold under such names as "Adelaide chinchilla"—have exposed it to massive trapping. In most states it is now protected for at least part of the year, but as recently as 1932, more than a million skins were exported in a season from New South Wales alone. In spite of the toll taken, the brushtails have remained plentiful everywhere—in back of the garden fence or in the outback of the mountain ranges. Unlike the ringtails, they range widely over the interior of the continent, nesting in deserted rabbit warrens or in box-tree eucalypts along dry creek beds. In suburban areas, they plague householders by nesting in attics, damaging roofs and staining ceilings. They have even been introduced into New Zealand, where they have prospered mightily in the face of a foreign flora and cold climate. To explain this mystifying adaptiveness, there is one slender clue. The brushtails are reported to eat a tremendous variety of plant food and even meat scraps. It may be, therefore, that they thrive because—like raccoons or opossums in America—they have the stomach for almost anything, including the refuse put out on the street.

Two last medium-sized possums deserve notice because they have striking black-and-white markings like those of a skunk. Also similar to skunks is their habit of giving off an evil stench, though they cannot throw their offensive scent as skunks can. Known as the striped possums (*Dactylopsila* and *Dactylonax*), or familiarly to some zoologists as just plain *Dax*, these creatures of the tropical rain forest are two-foot-long climbing animals. They are the most exclusively insectivorous of the possums, relying heavily on insects and larvae they find in dead wood. In hunting they are said to vibrate their sensitive paws over the bark to make the insects underneath disclose their presence. These they then feed on by ripping off the bark with long, rodentlike incisors or hooking them out by means of amazingly elongate fourth fingers and claws.

The smallest of the Australian phalangers are tiny pygmy or "dormouse" possums, no more than eight inches long, including three to four inches of tail. Pygmy possums spend their nights in pursuit of small insects through the treetops and pause occasionally to devour whole flowers—petals, pollen, nectar and all. Their relative, the tiny honey possum of southwestern Australia, has specialized in nectar eating, almost like a hummingbird or wasp. It raids the recesses of flowers by virtue of a long, hairy tongue, a probing, slender snout and a tubelike arrangement of the lips through which it can sip nectar even when hanging head down by its tail.

Corresponding with every size of possum, the phalangers have evolved gliding forms: pygmy gliders as small as pygmy possums; sugar gliders, squirrel gliders and yellow bellies, which weigh in with ringtails; and the greater glider, which is almost as large as a cuscus. The advantage of gliding, of course, is being able to forage extensively through stretches of broken forest without having to touch down between trees, where ground predators may be waiting. To this end all gliders have flat, loose-limbed bodies with membranes of skin running from wrist or elbow to ankle along their flanks, and fluffy or feathery tails that serve as rudders. Starting from the summit of one tree, they plane down through the air, often emitting what have been described as "bubbling shrieks" as they go, pulling up for a landing near the base of another tree. Then they climb the trunks they have reached to cull fresh harvests and go on to new glides.

Since they perform their stunts at night, they are more often heard than seen, but the greater glider can sometimes be made to leap in daylight if one pounds on its hollow-tree home with the blunt end of an ax. When the noise becomes intolerable, the big animal, sumptuously furred in brown or white, may poke its head from a hole in the trunk, waddle drowsily to the end of a limb and take off to find a quieter resting place.

The length of a glider's leap depends partly on the height from which it starts and partly on the size of its own body. The small, primitive pygmy glider makes prolonged leaps of perhaps a yard. The sugar and squirrel glider, by contrast, can glide 150 feet. The greater glider can sail over as much as 360 feet, dropping down within three feet of the ground. Each is seeking a slightly different kind of food. The pygmy gliders are out for insects and flowers. The middle-sized gliders fly in quest of many kinds of plant fare, plus insects and even mice. The greater glider is said to be almost totally vegetarian like the cuscus.

Among the phalangers is sometimes included the cuddlesome, Teddy-bearish koala, which plays the role of sloth or cuscus in *Eucalyptus* forests. This famous animal is unique, and taxonomists cannot agree as to how it should be classified. Apparently it has been shaped by one of the most extreme specializations of plant eating ever developed in a mammal.

Woolly, snub-nosed, round-eared, about 30 pounds in weight and about two and a half feet long when fully grown, the koala lives exclusively on *Eucalyptus* leaves—and more specifically on those of some 12 smooth-barked species, only a few of which are really preferred. To most other animals, these leaves are oily and poisonous. Seasonally new sprouts are so poisonous that even the koala must shift its attentions from one kind of tree to another.

To cope with its food, the koala has a stocking-shaped extension of its intestine, rather like an overgrown appendix, that measures six to eight feet long. It shelters in its gut a large population of symbiotic bacteria, which it passes on to its young in small wads of emulsified, half-digested *Eucalyptus* leaves.

The young themselves—probably because of the evolutionary refinements involved in growing up to be a successful koala—require an unusual amount of rearing. One or rarely two cubs are born to the female after some 32 to 35 days of pregnancy. They stay constantly in the pouch for about six months, intermittently for about three or four weeks more and then for a final month or two often ride pickaback in their mother's fur as she climbs and descends the *Eucalyptus* trees. Once weaned, they seldom if ever drink anything again except dew. Their name "koala" means "no drink" in one of the aboriginal dialects.

I T is something of a paradox that the koala's ability to utilize the most indigestible of all available plant foods has made it one of the most delicate and vulnerable of marsupials. Its digestive prowess does not extend to any other kind of foliage known. It must have *Eucalyptus* leaves or it dies. Moreover, its delicately balanced body chemistry apparently makes it extremely susceptible to viruses and bacteria brought to Australia by European men and animals. In precolonial Australia, there were enough *Eucalyptus* trees to support literally millions of koalas, but logging, trapping and epidemics had reduced them to thousands by the 1930s. Since then they have been carefully protected in sanctuary areas and are gradually being reintroduced into wild woodlands. Only in eastern Queensland have they survived in any numbers without special coddling.

The koala is tailless and has a backward-directed pouch which seems thoroughly inappropriate in an animal that is normally oriented head up on a tree trunk. The only reason suckling koala babies do not fall to the ground below is that they hold on tight with their mouths and are supported by maternal muscles that rim the door to their pouch home. For these and deeper anatomical reasons some zoologists feel that koalas originated from the same small arboreal forms which gave rise to the wombats and have only fairly recently gone back into the trees.

The wombats occupy a peculiarly isolated position on the tree of marsupial life. During damper times in the recent ice ages they had huge relatives in the now extinct *Dioprotodon* and *Nototherium*. They and their race have apparently been circumscribed by increased aridity in the last 20,000 years. But no

The mouse-sized honey possum of the southwestern coast of Australia differs from other possums in its preference for nectar. Its adaptations for this diet include a long snout and a long, narrow, pointed tongue. Hanging from a branch by its prehensile tail and opposable hind toes, it can extend its tongue an inch or more to probe a flower. The tip of the tongue is coated with tiny bristles (below) which pick up nectar and pollen as it is withdrawn. Needed protein is obtained from numerous tiny insects inadvertently picked up along with the nectar.

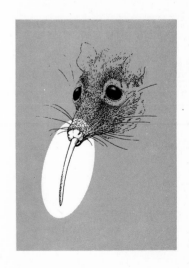

small primitive fossil forms have been found which might help to trace their descent. Anatomists say that they bear certain resemblances to the phalangers and must originally have stemmed from treetop creatures.

Living wombats, alone among marsupials, have many characteristics in common with rodents. They are chiefly night creatures, emerging after dark to graze on their favorite fodder, badger grass, or on several different kinds of roots. Some snuffle for a particular puffball fungus. Being gnawing animals, they have, like rodents, a single pair of large incisors in both upper and lower jaws. Their teeth are rootless, like those of rodents, and go on growing from within as fast as they are abraded from without. Wombats even look like rodents. To face one head on is to see a beaver. To glance at one from the side is to see a creature like a capybara. It has been suggested that the endemic Australian rodents replaced earlier marsupial animals. If they did—though the matter is entirely speculative—they most probably replaced the missing small wombats.

The dietary preferences of the wombats, though not as strict as some among Australian mammals, limit their range. Wombats are unknown in New Guinea or the arid interior of the mainland, but inhabit a broad strip of hill country from southern Queensland to Tasmania and a narrower strip west along the south coast as far as the Nullarbor Plain. In disrepute because of their destructive digging, they are still hunted in some areas as "badgers" or "ground hogs," and in the last century they were occasionally eaten as well. Ironically, their meat, according to one account, "somewhat resembles tough mutton."

THIS history of mammals offers no more dramatic example of a single model of animal radiating widely into many different categories of weight and environment than the incredible kangaroos. They come in all sizes, from tiny "squeakers" less than a foot high to giant-sized beasts that stand seven feet tall, measure up to nine feet from nose to tail and weigh more than 200 pounds. There are rat kangaroos, hare wallabies, *Dorcopsis* wallabies, tree kangaroos, rock wallabies, nail-tail wallabies, pademelon wallabies, true wallabies, stocky mountain euros, wallaroos and antilopines, and great gray foresters and desert reds. And all these many forms, large or small, are astonishingly similar—as like one another as they are unlike any other beast. No child from the streets of Chicago would be likely to mistake a kangaroo for an antelope, but not many native-born Australians can tell a nail-tail from a rock wallaby or a euro from other wallaroos.

No matter what its size, a typical kangaroo has small forelimbs, powerful hind limbs, immensely long slender hind paws and a muscular, tapered tail. Scientifically, kangaroos are known as macropods, which means "big feet." The great man-sized reds, foresters and mountain kangaroos, which fully live up to the popular image of what a kangaroo should be, belong to the genus *Macropus*. There is no basic difference between a kangaroo and a wallaby other than size, the kangaroo being larger and the wallabies smaller and more stocky. The name kangaroo itself derives from "gangaru," which in a north Queensland aboriginal dialect means small wallaby.

The ancestors of the kangaroos are thought to have descended from life in the treetops as diminutive ratlike offshoots of the phalanger stock. The most primitive surviving kangaroo is a small beast about 16 inches long and eight inches high, which lurks in the rain forest and moist dense brush of northeastern Queensland. It is known as *Hypsiprymnodon*, or the musky rat kangaroo. Alone of its race, the musky eats mainly insects and has a separate movable toe on each hind foot. Like some possums, it has an almost hairless tail covered with scaly skin. Like a bandicoot, it rummages in the earth for its living. Like a kangaroo, it has long hind feet and sturdy hindquarters, but it is said to walk on all fours like a rat.

In radiating from small ancestral forms such as the musky, the kangaroos have successfully taken to a great many different environments and ways of life. The medium-sized rock wallabies live almost exclusively in hilly country where they supplement their diet of grass with foliage, bark and roots. The slightly smaller *Dorcopsis* wallabies are tropical animals which browse and graze in the forests of the New Guinea region. The still smaller hare wallabies have acquired harelike habits. They crouch in well-formed "seats" in the grass, bound along with tremendous speed and generally live alone.

ONE of the most extraordinary adjustments of all has been made by the tree kangaroos, which have returned to arboreal life in the tropical forests of Queensland and New Guinea. In the process, though they have not regained the prehensile tails or grasping feet of their ancestors, they have changed considerably in other ways. Since they climb and leap more than they hop, they have little need for the enormous muscular tail of most kangaroos and have acquired instead a long slender tail useful as a balancing organ. Their forelimbs have not become shortened and are almost the same length as their hind limbs. Their forepaws are large and powerfully clawed for holding onto branches. Their feet have shortened and broadened and are treaded with ridged, nonskid pads. Using this equipment, they reportedly can climb ropes or drainpipes, can jump as much as 30 feet between trees and can leap down to the ground from limbs as high as 60 feet overhead. Such agility and bounce would be remarkable in a small animal; in a tree kangaroo, which may grow almost six feet long tip to tip, it is downright breathtaking.

While tree kangaroos browse on leaves high in the forest, the great majority of kangaroos eat mainly grass. They are the Australian counterparts of horses and cattle. And though they do not look like cattle, they possess similar teeth and intestines. They have sharp incisors for nipping off their fodder and broadly crowned, double-ridged molars for grinding it up. Their adult grinding teeth break through a pair at a time and gradually move forward in the jaw to replace earlier worn-out ones. Like cattle, they have a very long intestine and a sort of pseudo rumen which functions in somewhat the same way as the separate stomachs of ruminants by breaking down harsh vegetation in a gradual step-by-step sequence. Recent studies show that the first part of the intestine also serves, as does the more-developed rumen of cattle, to store half-chewed grass which is later thrown back into the mouth for chewing at greater leisure.

While foraging, the great red kangaroos of the interior plains usually associate in herds of from six to 50, known by Australians as "mobs." The word is most appropriate, because herd organization is almost nil. If one kangaroo in a mob is startled, it thumps its tail on the ground, alarming all the others, but there are no sentinels as such and no leaders. When the mob scatters, the kangaroos go off in random directions.

A kangaroo uses its big feet to move by a gait altogether unique in the circles of large animals. At a walk it puts down its forepaws and tail in a firm tripod and then swings both its heavy hind limbs forward together. At half speed its forepaws never reach the ground and its tail merely slaps down briefly. In full flight, traveling at up to 30 miles an hour, it holds both forepaws and tail high and bounces like a ball on the rippling rubber of its huge thighs.

Compared to the fully four-legged pacing of elephants or the galloping of horses, the kangaroo bounce is exhausting over a long distance but immensely effective in short bursts. By relaxing one leg and stiffening the other, a kangaroo can go off sideways, changing course in mid-career with an abruptness which baffles any ordinary quadruped that may be following it. In tussocky country, the artful dodging of small hare wallabies makes them almost impossible to catch even on horseback. The Australian field zoologist H. H. Finlayson once led an expedition in quest of a rare genus of rat kangaroo, *Caloprymnus*, long thought to be extinct. He found it surviving in the center in bare desert. With nowhere to hide, the tiny kangaroo, standing less than two feet high, exhausted three sets of mounts and ran 12 miles before it finally collapsed. Larger, heavier kangaroos are caught more easily in unobstructed country but, given hummocks and boulders, they too will outdodge anything but a bullet. One large kangaroo, at a single desperate bound, is reported to have cleared a pile of timber 10 1/2 feet high and 27 feet long.

In using their prodigious leaping powers, kangaroos appear to rely on instinctive stratagems which were probably evolved long ago in response to such beasts of prey as the marsupial wolf. When startled, a kangaroo bounds away explosively for a few dozen yards, then pulls up short to see if what flushed it merits further exertion. At this point an indifferent marksman can easily put a bullet through it. A second tactic—or perhaps a product of pure panic—is to double back, run directly toward a pursuer and unswervingly jump over his head. In this way, little hare wallabies have been known to clear full-grown zoologists. A female kangaroo with a large young one is said to make good her escape in a third way. When nearly spent, her pouch muscles apparently relax with the result that her baby falls out. Relieved of her burden, she bolts out of danger, returning for it later.

Though well equipped for running away, the large kangaroos are also capable of fighting successfully against almost all foes except fire, spear or bullet. When young, they are prey to eagles, dingoes and foxes. When adolescent, they learn in play how to grapple, hold and thrash about with their forepaws. This juvenile accomplishment has stood them in good stead in many a circus or prize ring where gloves have been tied on their forelimbs. But a mature unplayful way of fighting is far more dangerous than this "boxing" and has to be patiently curbed by handlers who train kangaroos as entertainers. Having gained a grip with a forepaw, an angry kangaroo can rear up on its tail and disembowel its antagonist with one rip of its huge, clawed hind feet. Many dogs and a few men have lost their lives from this knockout blow.

The big kangaroos adapt themselves easily to foreign climates and alien diets. They jump and spar in most zoos and half the circuses of the world. At home they once had few enemies or competitors, even in infancy, except the pouched wolf and a few of the birds and reptiles described in the next chapter. Today they have the dingo, the sheep, the camel, and most of all the farmer. Great red kangaroos and agile wallabies still graze in thousands over the central scrublands and northern savannas, but many of the others, such as the huge gray foresters or the diminutive hare wallabies, have become scarce. Up to now, no large grassland reserves have been set aside for them, and even in the arid heart of Australia, where the survivors remain most plentiful, the slaughter for dog food and shoe leather continues, posing a serious threat to their future.

A MOUSE-SIZED MARSUPIAL, THE FEATHER-TAILED GLIDER LIVES IN TREES, USING ITS BIG EYES AND ACROBATIC SKILL TO HUNT BUGS AT NIGHT

The Gentle Vegetarians

Among the marsupials, buck-toothed vegetarians comprise the largest and the most varied group. Phalangers, wombats and kangaroos subsist largely upon leaves and grasses. A few primitive, small phalangers also have added insects to their diet. Although not nearly as fierce as the carnivorous cats and wolves, they have survived much better. Many of them are still quite numerous.

THREE SUGAR GLIDERS, one munching on a grasshopper, hang in a she-oak. The widest-ranging phalangers, they live in coastal forests from New Britain to southeast Australia.

A MOUNTAIN POSSUM descends to the forest floor to feed at night. A rare 18-inch species, it keeps to high, heavily wooded regions where it is still avidly hunted for its fur.

The Possums: Bushy Acrobats

There are no monkeys in Australasia. Yet moving at night high in the trees of the New Guinea jungle and in the wild forests of the mainland are many four-footed, furry creatures with big, light-gathering eyes and long tails. These are the phalangers, or possums, which, unlike the American opossums, have the second and third digits of their hind feet bound together in a sheath of skin. This strong double toe, plus an opposable big toe like that of a monkey's, makes the phalangers particularly able tree climbers. Certain species, called gliders, have developed kitelike membranes similar to those of a flying squirrel, which enable them to sail through the air from tree to tree. Their glides are often accompanied by a racketing cry, which, because it is heard more often during the mating season, is thought to be the means by which these night creatures keep informed of each other's whereabouts. The small pygmy glid-

THE GREATER GLIDER is the best of the flying phalangers. In the air, with its gliding membrane stretched from front elbow to rear ankle, it looks like a kite with a long, furry tail.

THE CUSCUS, at 15 pounds, is the largest phalanger. Slow and drowsy by day, it is easily killed by native hunters, who find it by following down the foul, musky odor that it emits.

er makes brief leaps of a few yards, while the large sugar glider and the very large greater glider sail from 50 to 120 yards, sometimes dropping so close to the ground that they are occasionally caught by foxes.

The tails of most phalangers are prehensile, used to grip branches and carry nesting materials, but those of the gliders are bushy or featherlike and probably function as rudders for flight. By day,

phalangers sleep, often in family groups, curled up in the hollows of old trees, safe from predatory birds (though not from the long jaws of the tree goanna, a large, arboreal lizard). At dusk they awaken and start their search for food. The smaller species are insect eaters taking nectar and pollen from blossoms. Larger, slower forms, like the brushtail and cuscus, feed mainly on fruit and leaves, and may add to their diet with an occasional small animal.

STARTING A LEAP, A FIVE-INCH PYGMY POSSUM AIMS ITS BODY WHILE STILL GRIPPING A LEAF WITH THE PREHENSILE TOES OF ITS HIND FEET

IN MID-AIR (ABOVE) IT SPREADS ITS HANDLIKE PAWS JUST BEFORE LANDING (BELOW). IT EATS SMALL INSECTS AND EUCALYPTUS BLOSSOMS

Koalas: Built to Climb

Phascolarctos, the scientific name for the koala, means "pouched bear." At first glance that seems a fair description of this gentle, stump-tailed creature which drowses away its days up a tree. Anatomically, however, the koala is nothing like the omnivorous true bears. It eats only one food, the leaves of certain *Eucalyptus* trees, and its whole way of life is related to this diet. An adult, about the size of a large bulldog, consumes some two and a half pounds of these leaves a night—and nothing else. Indeed, the name koala is an aboriginal one meaning "no drink."

Because of its special diet, its low birth rate (the koala has one baby every other year), its disinclination to hide by day, its slow ways and the desirability of its soft fur, the koala was very hard hit by civilization. Twenty years ago it had been brought close to extinction. However, Australian conservationists have since reversed the trend, and the koala population is once again safe and growing.

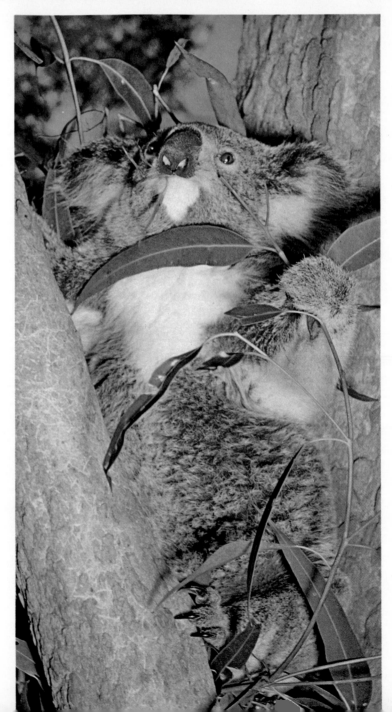

AT HOME on a branch, a koala displays the odd arrangement of its fingers, the first and second digits opposing the other three.

AT DINNER it feeds in the crotch of a eucalypt. The oily leaves of these gum trees require a highly specialized digestive system.

SUDDENLY FINDING ITSELF ALONE, A BABY KOALA LOOKS APPREHENSIVELY OVER ITS SHOULDER, LEAPS ACROSS TO ITS MOTHER AND CLIMBS T

LEADBEATER'S POSSUM, long believed extinct, was rediscovered in Victoria a few years ago. Its long, bushy tail, though not prehensile, helps it balance when climbing on slim boughs.

Getting Around in Trees

Phalangers are arboreal animals, many going from birth to death without ever touching the ground. As a group they are extraordinarily at home in their three-dimensional world and very well adapted to it. Their paws, both front and rear, have strong, clawed toes that are good at gripping. They have large eyes for night vision, and a variety of bushy or prehensile tails to aid them in gliding and climbing.

The early ancestors of this arboreal group are believed to have been small, agile insectivores rather like the pygmy possum on the opposite page. Scampering about the treetops, they apparently learned to lap nectar from blossoms and to supplement their diet of insects with the tender shoots of new buds. From this, it is believed, came the great radiation of the vegetarian marsupials, from the exclusively nectar-eating honey possum to the largest kangaroos, which came down from the trees ultimately to become the Australian equivalent of a gazelle.

THE BRUSH-TAILED POSSUM sleeps high up in trees and is a favorite food of native hunters, who locate their prey by the claw marks it leaves climbing up and down.

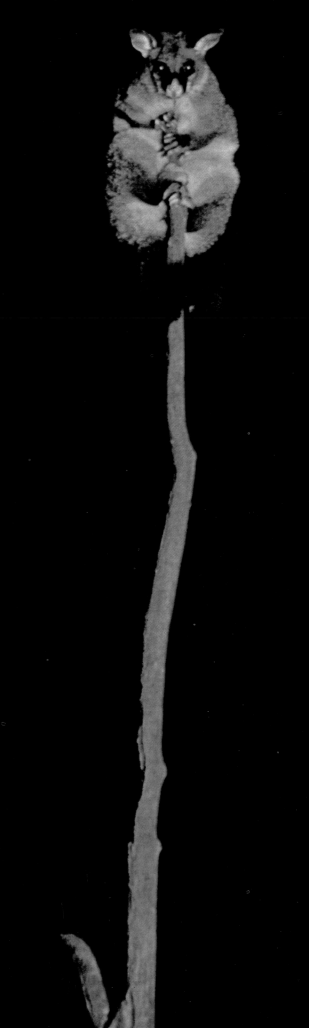

ARID INTERIOR. RED KANGAROOS GENERALLY LIE IN A SHADY SPOT DURING THE HEAT OF DAY AND MOVE OFF TO FEED IN THE LATE AFTERNOON

in dry open country. They are the best jumpers of all kangaroos and can cover 27 feet in one bound. Surprisingly, they are also fine swimmers. Lying flat in the water, they dog-paddle with their forelegs to keep their heads up, getting propulsion with kicks of their enormous hind legs. Adults weigh up to 200 pounds, or as much as a bull calf. They eat grass exclusively and compete directly with domestic livestock. Today, there are an estimated 100 million kangaroos and wallabies in Australia. In times of drought, they invade ranches, even airports. One herder recently shot 20,000 in two weeks.

117

From Boomers to Squeakers

While the phalangers were filling the treetops with a great variety of arboreal marsupial forms, the kangaroos exploded on the ground. Adapting their hopping gait to Australia's many different habitats, they produced species having a remarkable array of sizes and shapes. One kangaroo, after trying life on the ground for several million years, returned to the trees. Today, zoologists recognize some 45 different kinds, ranging in size from the big, male "boomers," the reds of the arid plains, down through the smaller hare-sized wallabies and the even smaller pademelons to the primitive little "squeakers," or rat kangaroos, which grub about in dank forest underbrush.

TASMANIAN BRUSH WALLABY

AGILE WALLABY
BRUSH-TAILED RAT KANGAROO

EURO, OR WALLAROO
RUFOUS RAT KANGAROO

TREE KANGAROO

PRETTY FACE WALLABY

SHORT-TAILED PADEMELON

RED-BELLIED PADEMELON

RINGED-TAIL ROCK WALLABY

BANDED HARE WALLABY

A BABY RED JOEY pulls open its mother's marsupium, or pouch, preparing to hop in. After some six months suckling in the pouch, there follows a six week period when the joey is weaned. It then begins feeding on grass and spends part of its time out on its own. A joey, even as big as the one above, will enter its mother's pouch headfirst and then turn itself around.

6

Deadly Snakes and Giant Lizards

IN Australia, as in every continent, the majority of animals belongs not to the mammal class but to more ancient lineages that were already well established before the mammals came. If we look back far enough into the murky past, we can imagine a time, about 400 million years ago, when Australia had no animals except crawling invertebrates and perhaps a few kinds of fishes confined to the fresh waters of its streams and lakes. Over the next 300 million years, this first fauna was enriched by all the main classes which preceded mammals in other lands: by insects, by spiders, by amphibians, by reptiles and by birds.

The few fossils found in Australia suggest that most of these groups established themselves down under at about the same time that they appeared in the world at large. In many places on the other continents it is possible to piece out a fairly continuous story of faunal succession by linking together fossils of increasing antiquity until a clear chain from primitive form to presently existing animal has been forged. In Australia this is not possible—for practically the entire last 65 million years, the known geological record is almost a total blank. As a result, the scientist has nothing but a small and perplexing scattering of remains to contemplate from the middle Cenozoic era and must jump from these directly into the present with its bewildering variety of living species.

The existing fauna is strange enough so that it deserves to have been chronicled better. Each major group of invertebrate or cold-blooded creatures is composed in an oddly assorted way that is distinctively Australian. For instance, the only species of amphibians in Australia are frogs and of those almost all belong to only two of the world's 18 frog families. The only turtles in Australia belong to a group unknown elsewhere except in South America. How account for such peculiarities of distribution? How read the story they may tell about the past? Such questions fascinate zoogeographers, and also tease them, because the answers are elusive and open to argument.

If we are denied knowledge of past history, we can at least study how the contemporary fauna compares on a world basis. When this is done, some very interesting and peculiar figures are revealed. To begin with, Australasia has only about six per cent of the earth's land; other things being equal, it should presumably have representatives of about six per cent of the world's species of animals. What it actually has is quite different: 17 per cent of the world's amphibians are represented in Australasia, 16 per cent of the world's insects, 14 per cent of the world's birds, 12 per cent of the world's reptiles and nine per cent of the world's mammals. In short, for its size Australasia is far richer in its variety of these creatures than it has any right to be. That is well worth thinking about, and we may as well start our thinking with the extraordinary richness of amphibians. Why amphibians? Why, of all creatures, those lowly frogs that are doing so badly elsewhere?

A very good question, and unfortunately one for which there is no present answer. The general abundance of life forms in the Australian geographic region is, at least in part, due to the fact that two radically different land masses are involved: dry, subtropical Australia and lush, tropical New Guinea, an island with mountain chains that have acted as isolating barriers and encouraged much speciation. In fact, the whole region abounds in islands and archipelagoes, many of these, like New Zealand, the Solomons, Bismarcks and Fiji, being themselves minor centers of speciation and radiation. Furthermore, the continent has been spared the severe ice ages and the extinctions that these must have caused in the Northern Hemisphere. By contrast, however, aridity must have been, and still remains, a factor in cutting back life in Australia. Even so, there have always been extensive stands of forest; as a result, Australia has come out "ahead" so far as variety goes.

I N any continent the first kinds of life to arrive have the advantage of diversifying in a competition vacuum, so to speak. It is they that have first chance to fill the innumerable ecological niches available. The fact that they have also been there longer has given them more time to develop a wide range of forms. Contrasting to this, however, are the effects of successive waves of better-adapted invaders. These are forms that have originated elsewhere and have brought with them innovations that are slightly advantageous. Accordingly, the history of the world's zoological evolution has been the arrival and radiation of one group, its suppression by a later intruder, which has in turn radiated, only to be overshadowed and, in its turn, overrun by a still better-adapted group. As noted, the long isolation of Australia has materially restricted the number of invaders reaching her shores. This means that the older endemic forms have not been challenged to the extent that earlier inhabitants of North America or Africa have. The survival and success of the marsupials in Australia bears out this.

Could it be said, as the above statistics suggest, that each successive class of vertebrates has succeeded the earlier one less completely in Australia than in the world at large? The high figures for amphibians as opposed to the less varied reptiles, birds and mammals seem to suggest this could be so. One should not, however, place too much importance on this. As we have seen, isolation and diversity of living conditions within the region favor a rich fauna. In the long run this is probably the really significant factor. Bearing this out is the fact that Australia's fresh-water fishes number only 4½ per cent of the world's species. Fishes are old, very old indeed, older even than amphibians. Why are they proportionately so scarce? There are two obvious reasons for this. First, fresh-water fishes cannot survive in the sea, and the fact that Australia is an island has discouraged immigration of fresh-water forms from the Asiatic continent. Australia has had to make do with whatever kinds it could develop on its own. This brings us to the second point: the dryness of Australia. In a continent whose rivers have, for millions of years, been few, short, shallow and prone to dry up, obviously fishes as a group will not prosper.

So much, then, for statistics. What about the flesh-and-blood creatures themselves? The fresh-water fishes, amphibians and reptiles will be taken up later in this chapter, but first the insects and spiders deserve a passing glance.

Australasia has more than its share of insects: nearly 50,000 described species on the mainland and an estimated 65,000 more on the islands. If these teeming hordes are analyzed group by group and compared with the same groups in the world as a whole, it turns out that Australia itself is relatively rich in highly evolved forms of insect life and relatively poor in primitive types. This surprising up-to-dateness actually fits in well with what is known of insect history all over the world. Entomologists generally feel all basic types of insects were on earth by the end of the Cretaceous period, when Australia is presumed to have become isolated. New Zealand, probably having been isolated much longer, presents a different picture. It is relatively rich in such primitive insects as springtails and relatively poor in advanced forms such as ants or butterflies.

From studying Australian insects, many entomologists believe that once, in the Mesozoic, there were land connections between Australia, South America, India and perhaps even Africa. Current zoological thinking tends to discredit such land bridges, but it is worth considering an example that shows why they were originally envisaged. As pointed out by J. W. Evans of the Australian Museum, a certain genus of large primitive blepharocerid fly called *Edwardsina* occurs only in Australia, Tasmania and South America. There it lives only in the cascades of waterfalls or under the rocks of fast-flowing streams. So shackled is the creature to the fresh water in which it lives that close students of insects cannot imagine how it could have spread from one continent to the other except by going from stream to stream along a continuous belt of dry land.

There are scores of other Australian insects, like *Edwardsina*, which have their closest kin in South America—also some fresh-water fishes, frogs, land turtles and plants. Possibly some of these creatures have crossed from one continent to another through freak accidents of wind and weather. Possibly some of them are relics of populations which were once distributed globally. Or possibly at some time before the Cretaceous period, Australia and South America actually were connected. Of many ancient Mesozoic land links which have been proposed for Australia, this one retains a wide following among zoologists and may be justified by the evidence.

While the majority of Australian insects is of ordinary size, the region contains a number of interesting giants. The continent boasts a form of silverfish-like insect that grows two inches long; an archaic dragonfly, five and a half inches across the wings, that is said to fly at 60 miles per hour; several mantis-like stick insects 10 inches across the wings and 10 inches long; a huge primitive termite more than an inch long; an enormous biting, stinging ant of equal length—the bulldog—which is something to avoid in Australian gardens; the world's largest earwig, measuring two inches; the world's largest thrips, measuring half an inch; one-and-a-half-inch jewel beetles so lustrous that they are often set like precious stones in brooches and pendants.

New Zealand has a three-inch weevil and a curious camel cricket known as a weta. The ordinary weta is a solidly built insect two inches long. Its cousin, the cave weta, runs to a more spindly daddy longleg frame but spans as much as 14 inches as it stands on dark cavern walls. One of the world's largest butterflies, *Papilio alexandrae*, is a bird-wing of the Solomon Islands that flaps about on nearly a full foot of wing span.

WHAT are these huge forms? Are they simply products of a favorable environment? Or are they the giant survivors at the twig-ends of bygone insect radiations? We do not know. Giant insects were once common on earth during the Pennsylvanian period, some 300 million years ago. It may be that certain primitive genetic tendencies, plus certain competitive and environmental factors, have combined to allow some giants to persist among Australian insects today.

Despite the over-all up-to-dateness of the insect fauna, it nevertheless includes a number of extremely primitive forms found nowhere else. New Zealand abounds in tiny archaic flies. Its micropterygid moths, no more than one fourth to one half an inch in wing span, show traces of fly anatomy in their make-up, which lead them to be classified as the most primitive lepidoptera known. Australia's flower wasps fill a gap between primitive digger wasps and the more advanced social wasps. The female flower wasp has no wings. She simply lurks on the ground and, as the male shuttles past en route from one low blossom to another, grabs him in her huge mandibles and takes a ride with him. After a brief flight she drops off, rummages into the earth and finds a scarab beetle larva. This she stings, paralyzing it into an insensible mass of potential food and covering it with the eggs of her voracious progeny.

The giant one-inch Australian termite, *Mastotermes*, intrigues naturalists because it combines the most primitive known wing venation with the most primitive known termite social organization. Other termites are noted for their complex caste systems of queens, kings, soldiers, workers and nymphs, each of which develops differently and plays a different role in termite society. In the smallish two-foot underground nests of *Mastotermes*, the males and females look much alike and no one yet has been able to find a queen. The creature is a typical termite, however, in its wood-eating habits, and immensely successful and destructive all through tropical Australia. It has been known to eat through lead piping and on one occasion to reduce a set of billiard balls to neatly hollowed-out shells.

Both Australia and New Zealand shelter a unique group of fungus gnats, the diadocidianae, which hang as larvae on cave walls and glow like fireflies. Their eerie clusters make the Waitomo Caves in New Zealand and the Bundanoon Caverns of New South Wales world-famous tourist attractions.

Of spiders, Australia has a normal complement—which is rather surprising, since spiders are wingless. Instead, young spiders go kiting on the wind, using their webs as sails and reaching altitudes of 25,000 feet or more. Others make passage on drifting logs. So effective are their methods of world travel that many Australian spider species belong not only to families, but even to genera known widely in other lands as well. The black widow genus, *Latrodectus*, for instance, is represented by a single species which ranges from Arabia to southern Asia and Australia. It is called the red-back or red-spot in Australia, the katipo in New Zealand.

Both red-back and funnel-web (*Atrax*) are poisonous, but the rest of Australia's spiders are relatively harmless and do a Herculean share in the work of insect control. The big four-inch huntsman spiders, *Isopoda* and *Delena*, for example, are often tolerated, sometimes even encouraged, as residents in country homesteads. Veterans of the outback are apt to tell tenderfeet they always keep a huntsman spider in their nets at night to eliminate the inevitable mosquito that gets in. Of the great orb weaver genus *Nephila*, the female, spanning seven or eight inches, spins webs so sturdy that she can catch small birds in them; so sturdy, indeed, that the Melanesian natives collect them to use as dip nets and gill nets in fishing. The magnificent spider has dispensed with the full routine of web stringing and hangs out a single silken thread, baited at the end with a glob of glue. Should a moth inspect this whirling lure, the female spider secures her meal by a twitch of one of her eight feet. She is known appropriately as one of the spider anglers.

None of the animal classes of Australia is more suggestive of the continent's long isolation than the fishes which swim in its streams. Seemingly, fresh-water fishes are free to come and go wherever there is water, but in actual fact the majority of them can no more enter brine and survive there than they can come out and walk on dry land. As a result, they cross ocean barriers even less readily than many terrestrial animals.

Australia has only 180 kinds of fresh-water fishes—fewer than any other continent. Furthermore, of these 180, only two are "primary" and all the rest are "secondary." Primary fresh-water fishes are those which have no close relatives living in salt or brackish water today and no taint of salt in their fossil relatives of the past. They came into fresh-water rivers from the sea before they were fishes, and did their evolving there. "Secondary" fresh-water fishes, on the other hand, are those clearly derived from ocean-going lineages; their ancestors went back to the sea from the rivers, as did all salt-water fishes, but some returned to fresh water a second time.

WHY did fish evolve in fresh water? This is not known. But it has been suggested that the advantage of having mobility in swift currents and, along with it, the ability to escape the clutches of huge aquatic scorpions called eurypterids, may have been factors which led to the development of a type of animal with supple backbone, muscular body and tail fin. This was about 450 million years ago.

The only two primary fresh-water fishes in Australia are *Scleropages* and *Neoceratodus*. *Scleropages* is a large fish, two to three feet long, which swims in streams of the New Guinea and Queensland region. Its known fossil lineage does not go back as far as the Cretaceous and there is some doubt as to whether it is a true primary type or an early secondary type which could have come through the ocean. *Neoceratodus*, on the other hand, is one of the most ancient

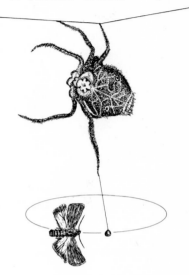

A "FISHING" SPIDER

Unlike most spiders, which trap their prey in webs, the hairy imperial spider angler "fishes" for its food. To do this it first spins a horizontal thread from which it hangs. Then it lowers another thread, tipped by a sticky droplet, and swings it in a circle waiting for an insect to pass. It is not certain whether the insect is attracted by the motion of the lure or by an odor emitted by the spider. In any case, the insect gets stuck to the whirling globule and is hauled in.

A ONCE-A-YEAR BREEDER

The corroboree toad lives in a cold environment high in the mountains. Like most other amphibians, it needs water for the development of its eggs. These are laid in summer either on damp sphagnum moss or under the snow, there being little or no standing water in its harsh environment during most of the year. Sooner or later it rains, or there is an unseasonal thaw, and the eggs are washed into temporary puddles where they pass through the tadpole stage and emerge as toads. If the rain or thaw is delayed—sometimes for five months—the embryos will begin to develop into tiny toads right in the eggs.

and "primary" fresh-water fishes known. It is a lungfish, a close relative of the crossopterygian fishes, among which were the ancestors of the amphibians.

Back in the Devonian period, some 350 million years ago, lungfish and crossopterygians both frequented inland continental waters where, it is thought, they were sometimes imprisoned in stagnant pools or left high and dry on mud flats. Both developed the ability to gulp air into primitive lungs—into the sacs which were to evolve as the gas bladders in most other fishes. The crossopterygians, because of an arrangement of their fin bones, went on to acquire the knack of trundling across mud bars.

These fins are believed to have eventually become legs, and they probably connect the crossopterygians with all vertebrate land animals from frogs to men. Most of the lungfishes, meanwhile, merely perfected their ability to hole up in parched mud banks. One modern African species has proved capable of surviving out of water for as long as four years. The three other African and the one South American species all have similar habits. They all estivate in cocoons of dried mud, they all have two lungs and they all need occasional gulps of air. If held underwater long enough, they drown. By contrast, the brawny six-foot Australian *Neoceratodus* has only one lung, never needs to surface in well-aerated running water, and never, so far as is known, hides out in parched mud. It has survived merely as a very ancient, very "primary" fresh-water fish, confined to two small rivers in southeastern Queensland: the Mary and the Burnet.

Fossils show that *Neoceratodus* has had relatives in Australia for at least 200 million years. Has all of its evolutionary development and history been in Australia or, way back, did its ancestors go through a period in the sea? Most students of fishes believe it has always been a creature of fresh water and look upon it as the one most persuasive piece of evidence that Australia had a complete bridge of land, veined with streams, leading to some other part of the globe. Others, perhaps more realistically, feel that salt tolerance or intolerance cannot be projected so far back into the past.

The Australasian amphibians are all frogs, there being no salamanders. The frogs are remarkable as a group because of the astonishing adaptations some of them have made to inhospitable environments. Most amphibians need water in which to lay their eggs, but the most primitive Australasian frogs, the mountain-dwelling *Leiopelma* of New Zealand, lay their eggs under rocks and logs. When the young ones hatch, they drag tails behind them like tadpoles, but they walk on dry land. Although these tails are absorbed in the first four weeks of life, adult leiopelmids never lose their tail-wagging muscles as other frogs do.

A second group of leiopelmids—so classified—lives in the cold mountain headwaters of the American Northwest. It resembles the New Zealand group in having primitive bone structure. But it lays its eggs in water and goes through a more or less normal adolescence as a tadpole.

THE frogs of the Australian mainland, though they come of more recent stock than the New Zealand *Leiopelma*, are dominated by two very ancient groups, some members of which have adapted themselves to arid sectors of the continent. The older group of the two, the leptodactylids, seems both figuratively and literally to be very deeply entrenched in the environment. That is, they occupy highly specialized niches of life and in many cases they escape drought by actually digging deep into the earth. During the dry season in New South Wales, the Catholic frog, so named for a crosslike marking on its back, springs up out of the earth after every shower, gorges itself on insects, mainly termites, and then disappears into the ground again as the puddles dry. One of its close kin, the corroboree toad, occupies the extreme opposite in habitats. It lives above the 4,500-foot level in the Mount Kosciusko area, where it is buried by snow for four or five months every year.

The water-holding frog *(Cyclorana)*, inhabiting the dry, arid regions of the interior, distends its body with water so that it comes to resemble a small tennis ball. As the water holes and creeks dry up, it burrows beneath the mud, and there, surrounded by dry mucus, it awaits the next rain. Aborigines dig them up for the water they contain and also for food. Other frogs, too, escape drought by burrowing.

The other large group of frogs, the *Hyla*, while largely arboreal, has a few desert dwellers too. They survive "in the deserts of central Australia . . . not by burrowing, but by very rapid reproduction and dispersal from one water hole to another when rain occurs," according to Philip J. Darlington, Jr., the noted zoogeographer.

Actually relatively few species of frogs live in the dry regions of Australia. Ninety per cent of them inhabit areas that have an average rainfall of more than 25 inches, making possible for them the "normal" kind of frog life typical of the group elsewhere in the world.

Australasia supports more than its quota of reptiles and they are interestingly diverse. But again there are various gaps. The stocks of animals that are missing—further evidence of the region's long isolation—are almost as significant as the turtles, crocodiles, lizards and snakes which are actually present. There are no snapping turtles, no common turtles, no side-necked turtles, no soft-shelled turtles except a single newcomer in New Guinea; there are no vipers, pit vipers or rattlesnakes.

T HE kinds of reptiles which actually have chanced to reach Australasia fall into three main categories: those with close kin nowhere else in the world, those with close kin mainly in South America, and those with close kin mainly in Asia. The members of the first two groups may sprout from branches lower on the tree of reptilian life than those of the last group and have probably lived in Australasia the longest. How long no one really knows, but it is possible that creatures similar to the present Australian turtles or the New Zealand tuatara have been in residence for as many as 200 million years.

The only Australasian reptiles which have no living relatives elsewhere are an inscrutable orphan of the turtles known as the "New Guinea pitted-shell," 14 species of queer little legless lizards called pygopodids, and the tuatara. Saw-tooth-tailed, more than two feet long and superficially lizardlike, the tuatara still manages to survive on a few islands off the New Zealand coast as the last member of the reptile order Rhynchocephalia, which came into being before the dinosaurs had vanished in all other parts of the globe about 135 million years ago.

The legless Australian pygopodid lizards, which move and look very like snakes, lack a forked tongue and usually have a pair of large scales projecting from the sides of the body, vestigial remains of hind legs. Since lizards, but not snakes, discard tails when struck, an even easier, if cruder, way to identify a pygopodid is to hit it. The part streaking for its burrow or its refuge in the grass is the main animal. The tail, often more than twice the length of the head and body, is the part left behind.

Of the "South-America-related" reptiles in Australasia, the most important

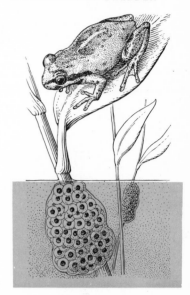

Widely distributed in Australia, the brown tree frog is found wherever there is water. Unlike the corroboree toad, which lays only a dozen eggs, this one attaches a cluster of two or three hundred to a grass stalk in any convenient stream or pond. These eggs develop very quickly, hatching in a few days and turning into frogs seven weeks later—a useful adaptation for this species, since Australian ponds tend to dry up. As soon as the frogs are grown they are ready to mate. If it rains, they will do so immediately, but in drier parts of their range, they may wait for months before they are able to reproduce.

are the turtles—the majority of which belong to a primitive aquatic family, the snake-necks, or chelyids—and a genus of small handsome iguanid lizards that lives on the Fiji and Tonga islands.

The 13-odd species of Australian turtles, or tortoises, as they are called in Australia to distinguish them from the large sea turtles that breed on offshore coral islands, are all fresh-water inhabitants. The best known of the tortoises are the long-necks, a species that abounds in coastal marshes, and the Murray tortoise, the very common inhabitant of the inland waterways. Both consume aquatic insects and mollusks, and their ability to leave a drying marsh and find a wet one places them at a big advantage over fishes. During such untimely migrations they may be killed by the dozens as they cross roads, or by the hundreds against impenetrable wire fences. Though they live out most of their lives in water, these tortoises lay their eggs on land, digging a hole in sand or soil above the waterline and leaving it for the sun to bring forth the young.

Tortoises form one of the favorite foods of the Australian aborigines, the women wading through the swamps and groping for them with their hands. The early European settlers pronounced the Murray tortoise as "good eating" but said that the long-neck "stank horribly."

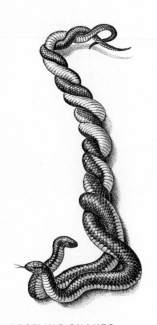

WRESTLING SNAKES

Though many snakes wrestle, the Australian brown snake is exceptional in the extremes of coiling to which it goes. Two males of similar size, each apparently bent on dominating the other, will line up side by side, then quickly throw coils over each other's body until they are wound together as closely as a two-strand rope. Hissing and writhing, they continue to twist and squeeze until both are exhausted. They then uncoil, and the beaten snake moves away. These contests are apparently concerned with territorial dominance. It was once thought that they had to do with mating, until observers noticed that females were never involved.

THE world distribution of the iguanid lizard is very peculiar. Most of them inhabit the American tropics, whence few have worked their way south as far as Tierra del Fuego and to the Galápagos Islands 600 miles off the coast of Ecuador. But two mysterious genera crop up on the island of Madagascar off the coast of Africa. How did these animals get to Madagascar and to the Fiji Islands? Did they swim; did they come across Antarctica on some ancient land bridge? Or do they survive in these far outposts because they have not yet been supplanted by another group of lizards, the agamids? The agamids are common elsewhere in the world, and as the supposed evolutionary descendants of the iguanids, are believed to have exterminated them everywhere else. The answer, if it is ever to be found, still lies buried among the earth's undug iguanid fossils.

Some Australasian reptiles have their closest family ties in Eurasia. The fresh-water crocodiles of New Guinea and northern Australia are slender-nosed types similar to those found in rivers throughout the Indo-Malayan region. They live upstream from the much larger man-eating, seagoing crocodiles that range the Indian Ocean and western Pacific.

Except for the iguanids of the Fijis and Tongas, Australasian lizards come of Asiatic or cosmopolitan lineages. Indeed the colonization of Australasia by Asiatic reptiles continues even now, for many New Guinea geckos and skinks are similar or identical to Asiatic types. The New Zealand geckos are unusual in that they bear their young alive. The blue-tongued *Tiliqua* skink of Australia grows as much as two feet long, exceeds all others of its family in sheer size. One large skink of the Solomons, *Corucia*, has developed a sturdy prehensile tail—thereby flouting the normal skink law that tails are for losing while confusing pursuers.

One of the oddest of the skink lizards is the stumpy-tail, whose unusually large scales overlap like the tiles of a roof. This resident of the interior of southern Australia has a rounded tail the same shape as the head, a body structure which has earned it the schoolboy's nickname of double-headed lizard. Its protection against predators is virtually complete: few potential enemies maintain interest long enough to fight their way through its armor.

The oldest and most impressive lizards of Australasia are the great predatory monitors. They have physical features suggestive of the fossil ancestors
of the snakes on the one hand, and of the huge Cretaceous sea-monster moso-
saurs on the other. Today there are 24 monitor species known in the world;
of these, 15 are found in Australasia. The largest is the 10-foot Komodo dragon
of Komodo Island in the East Indies. The Australian perentie runs it a close
second at over eight feet. Fossils reveal that only a few hundred thousands of
years ago some Australian monitors stretched over 15 feet. By contrast the
modern Australian deserts harbor little burrowing monitors less than 18
inches long.

Known down under as goannas, the monitors have long claws, forked
tongues like snakes, voracious meat-eating dispositions, and dazzling abilities
as runners and climbers. The great eight-foot perentie of the north and center
is now scarce, but the six-foot goanna still holds out successfully, especially
in the eastern forest regions. When surprised out in the open, it makes for
the nearest upright—which may be the nearest leg of a terrified man or horse.
Once so "treed," it is difficult to detach without exacting an ounce of flesh in
the process.

One other group of lizards vies with the monitors as a distinctive element
in the Australian scene. This is the agamids, the supposed successors of the
iguanids. They are known locally as "dragon lizards," and though not as big
as monitors, they fully deserve the name because of their spiny ugliness and
their frightening mechanisms of bluff and bluster. The northern frill-neck,
when alarmed, suddenly opens a violently colored parasol of skin on either
side of its throat. The little "devil" of the desert, *Meloch horridus*, bristles
with spines. The big, common bearded dragon changes color tone and bubbles
out the skin of its neck in a large Adam's apple. The diminutive white salt
dragon pursues tiny black ants on the 4,000 square miles of dry Lake Eyre's
salt pan. For protection against the glare, its sunken eyes are visored by long,
serrated eyelids. Its nostrils are little more than tiny slits as a filter against the
blowing salt. For camouflage against aerial reconnaissance, its back is as blanched
as the bones of a *Diprotodon*.

GRAPPLING GOANNAS

*Male goannas also fight, but their style
of combat is quite different—they battle
with tooth, claw and tail. After some
gulps of air, throat swelling and loud
hissing preliminaries, they rear up on
their hind legs and close in. The final
outcome of the contest is usually decided
by the goanna's most effective weapon,
its muscular tail, which in a seven-foot
lizard is about four feet long. This can
be lashed out with a force sufficient to
knock a man over or break a dog's legs.*

T HE snake situation in Australia is as puzzling as almost everything else
down under—mostly because of the profusion of one group that should be
scarce and the relative scarcity of another group which should be more numerous. The first snakes to evolve in the world at large were the pythons. In
due course they found their way to Australia, where they are commonest in the
north. The largest of the group, the amethystine, grows up to 24 feet long
and is able to swallow wallabies.

From the ancestors of the pythons evolved an important and widespread
group of snakes, the colubrids. These include many of the commonest snakes
now found in most parts of the world, but surprisingly, they are represented
in Australia by a handful of only 14 species. From colubrids, in turn, developed two groups of poisonous snakes, the front-fanged elapids (the cobras,
kraits, coral snakes and mambas), and the folding-fang vipers and pit vipers
(rattlers, copperheads, water moccasins, etc.). These large groups of poisonous
snakes are believed by herpetologists to represent the latest branchings from
the snake line. Therefore, if Australia is to be regarded as the place where
more primitive forms have radiated widely in isolation, then it is logical to
assume that newcomers like the elapids and vipers should either be absent

from the continent or at least fairly rare. As far as the vipers are concerned, logic is borne out; there is not a single one in all of Australia. But there are 70 species of elapids—a larger proportion of venomous snakes than any other continent in the world. As far as is known, there is absolutely no explanation for this. They have obviously been there for a long time, to judge by their variety and by the way they have penetrated into every corner of the land. But how they got there and how they did it *before* their more primitive relatives are not known.

Australia has some of the most poisonous snakes in the world, but it also has some large but harmless species which are helpful to man. The carpet snake (*Morelia variegata*) and the incongruously named children's python (*Liasis childreni*) both prey on rats and rabbits, animals which have plagued Australia since the white settlement. Both snakes grow to a length of about seven feet, both have a pale yellow undersurface and both are widely distributed across the country. Farmers recognize the control these snakes exercise on the rodent and rabbit population and permit them on their farms despite their startling size.

Most of the venomous species are less than lethal to human beings, but a half dozen of them can kill, and at least one, the taipan, kills almost invariably. The sometimes deadly species include the so-called Australian "copperhead," *Denisonia;* the short, stout *Acanthophis*, known comfortingly as the "death adder"; the brown snake, *Demansia*, and the black snake, *Pseudechis*, both of which are known for the wrestling matches their males put on in springtime for territorial rights and female favors.

Another feared killer is the six-foot tiger snake, whose fangs exude one of the most potent toxins ever tested. The enormous taipan's venom may not be quite as strong but it is much more plentiful. When milked, a single tiger snake is said to have produced enough poison to kill 118 sheep, and the big taipan enough for 200 lethal doses. This compares with dosage sufficient for 31 sheep, extracted from the Indian cobra, or for eight sheep, taken from the U.S. copperhead.

FORTUNATELY the taipan is a rare, retiring forest creature which would much rather run than strike. Until the development of antivenom serums, the tiger snake probably took more lives because it is fairly common throughout Australia. The absolute awesomeness of the taipan, however, is unrivaled except by the 18-foot king cobra of tropical Asia. In 1950 a young zoologist, Kevin C. Budden, while out collecting in Queensland, caught a taipan and successfully wrestled it back to his car. Shoving it into a bag, he was bitten by its half-inch fangs. His companions were kept from killing it only by his insistence that it should be sent back alive to the Commonwealth Serum Laboratories in Melbourne to be milked. The next day, despite all the most modern medical precautions that could be taken, he was dead.

For reasons unknown, the swift neurotoxins of the taipan and tiger are apparently ineffective against the largest monitor lizards. A deep enmity exists between these two closely related reptile groups, which must reach far back into the past. Given a goanna and a dangerous elapid, one is apt to see a close battle to the finish—one from which the goanna staggers away overfed and groggy, digesting poison, but usually victorious. No other Australian predators—not the marsupial wolf, not the placental dingo, not the birds of prey— can stand up to the poisonous elapids as brazenly and live to see the next sunrise.

TERMITES ARE AMONG THE MOST COMMON AUSTRALIAN INSECTS. ONE SPECIES BUILDS CLAY-COVERED, HONEYCOMBED NESTS 20 FEET TALL

The Lower Animals

Among the ranks of cold-blooded animals in Australia are many strange creatures, including foot-long insects and eight-foot lizards, spiders that cast nets over passing flies, giant snakes that swallow kangaroos whole, frogs that climb trees and hide under the bark, and others that live and breed in desert areas, although they are dependent upon water throughout their entire life cycle.

THE LONG-HORNED GRASSHOPPER HAS ANTENNAE THAT ARE FREQUENTLY LONGER THAN ITS BODY. LIVING MOSTLY IN THE HIGHEST BRANCHES

FRESH FROM ITS NYMPHAL CASE, a female double drummer cicada pauses on a trunk while its wings fill out and harden. This species takes up to six years to mature underground.

The Insects

Australia is known to have about 50,000 different kinds of insects, but there may be many more, since entomologists feel that not all the existing species have been described. Not all are as big as the double drummer at left, or as noisy. This cicada has a wingspread of five inches, and the male is equipped with a pair of "drums," or membranes, larger than in any other cicada. Located at the junction of the abdomen and thorax, these conceal other membranes, parchmentlike in texture, which, when vibrated rapidly, produce a humming sound—the love song of the cicada. Curiously, the female cannot hear, thus the song must go unheard, although not unfelt; her body picks up the vibrations. These attract her to the source and stimulate her into mating behavior. A similar song may have been among the first animal sounds heard on earth. The cicada has an evolutionary history going back 250 million years, and fossils found in Australia show how little some of the living species have changed.

A BORDERLINE INSECT, the regent skipper is classified as a butterfly, although the male exhibits qualities of a moth. Bristles on its rear wings fit into sockets on the forewings and lock both together for more efficient flight—a characteristic of most moths. This helps to set the regent apart not only from other Australian skippers, but from all other butterflies.

A FUNNEL-WEB SPIDER PEERS FROM ITS NEST. FOR ITS SIZE IT IS ONE OF THE WORLD'S DEADLIEST ANIMALS: ITS VENOM CAN KILL A MAN

Killing with Fang and Net

Of the 1,500 known varieties of spiders in Australia, only three are deadly, and of these, the deadliest is the funnel-web spider shown above. Its needle-like fangs, longer and more effective than those of many snakes, transmit a venom that has claimed 10 human lives since 1927. The assassin spider (*opposite*) is also poisonous, but of no danger to humans—belonging to a group more famous for their hunting techniques than their bite. One species of assassin tosses its web-net over its victim, gladiator fashion. Another hangs its net from threads, and by manipulating them like a puppeteer, manages to flick both net and itself in the way of passing insects. This happens so quickly that scientists have not yet figured out how the spider manages to do it.

A RED DESERT SCORPION, a distant relative of the spiders, brings its tail and poison stinger into striking position. Weak-eyed, it must feel its way in the desert with its sensitive claws.

AN ASSASSIN SPIDER crawls nimbly over a plant, aided by long legs. These spiders make new webs nightly. With the coming of dawn, they dismantle them; some eat the threads.

Amphibians High and Dry

With more than half of the continent arid, it is not surprising that the majority of Australia's frogs and toads should be found crowded into the few regions that get 25 inches or more of rain a year. What is startling is that some successfully inhabit desert areas with an annual rainfall of less than 10 inches, since, like most other amphibians, they need water in which to lay their eggs and raise their young. They survive in deserts primarily because they do not have a regular mating season, as do other frogs; instead, they are opportunistic breeders—mating whenever sufficient rain has fallen to form ponds and pools. Moreover, their tadpoles develop faster than do those in wetter regions, coming to maturity before the ponds have dried up.

As a protection against heat and drought, desert frogs and toads retreat underground, often remaining there in little cells for months at a time and re-emerging after the next rain. One species digs through sand to reach the cool, moist subsoil, 26 to 33 inches below the hot surface, but others, impeded by the hard clay, can go down only 12 inches. Some take a supply of water with them into their burrows, stored in their swollen bodies. Aborigines catch these frogs in droughts and sometimes get as much as a mouthful of water by squeezing them.

PERON'S TREE FROG, LIKE OTHERS OF ITS KIND, HAS WEBBED DIGI

THE CORROBOREE TOAD, shown on a bed of sphagnum moss, lives at altitudes of 4,500 or more feet. Rarely seen, it is a burrower and was not described by scientists until 1953.

THE SPHAGNUM FROG, like the corroboree toad, dwells at high altitudes, lacks webbing between its digits and lays its eggs in the sphagnum. The tadpoles mature in the wet moss.

THE TURTLE FROG has heavy forelegs with which it burrows into the ground headfirst, the only frog to do so. It is found living with termites in sandy soil, often at a distance from water.

A FROG OF THE RED CENTER, *Neobatrachus centralis* sits hip deep in a rare puddle. It lives in a shallow burrow, which it digs in the shadow of shrubbery for protection against the desert sun.

THE AMETHYSTINE PYTHON, a 24-foot-long invader from New Guinea, is the biggest Australian snake. It has been known to bolt down whole kangaroos weighing as much as 50 pounds.

THE DEATH ADDER is one of Australia's most poisonous snakes. Three feet long, it has a nine-inch range and strikes accurately. One out of every two of its human victims dies.

The Reptiles

No other continent has so large a proportion of venomous snakes as Australia: more than 70 of its 130 species are poisonous. Luckily, as with most snakes elsewhere, none of these strikes at humans unless provoked, and not all have a lethal bite. The death adder, whose venom is 10 times more powerful than that of its cousin, the king cobra, uses its tail as a lure, wiggling it in front of its mouth and enticing small animals within striking range.

Once struck, the victim dies of asphyxiation, the venom causing paralysis of the muscles that control breathing. Protective coloration and its ability to remain motionless make the death adder difficult to spot, and people have stepped on it without realizing it was there.

Lizards are fairly well represented in Australia, and although none are poisonous, some, like the lace, or tree, monitor (*below*), can be fearsomely big.

A LACE MONITOR, which may grow as long as six feet, takes a bluffing stance. Largely arboreal in habit, it runs up anything resembling a tree, even the legs of horses, when frightened.

A BLUE-TONGUED SKINK puts out its tongue and spreads its body in an attempt to look fierce. It feeds on insects, birds and mice, and gives birth to living young, often as many as 12.

7

The Birds
of Down Under

A<small>N</small> eagle sailing in the desert sky over Alice Springs; a hundred thousand nod-
dies nesting in the *Pisonia* trees of a remote Barrier Reef inlet; a single
flock of over a hundred million migrating muttonbirds, their numbers carefully estimated by Captain Matthew Flinders off Tasmania about 1800; an old
map on which Australia is labeled "*Terra psittacorum*" (Land of Parrots)—
these glimpses of down under give a true over-all picture: that Australia has
been, and still is, a paradise for feathered settlers.

In proportion to its size, Australasia today supports more than twice as many
bird species as North America. Not counting sea birds and seasonal visitors,
ornithologists recognize altogether 1,212 bird species for the Australasian region. Of these, over half belong to families based in Asia and may be assumed
to have come down the Malaysian island chains in the last several millions of
years. All the rest belong not merely to endemic species, or even genera, but to
entire endemic families and subfamilies—to whole categories of groups of related birds which occur nowhere else on earth.

How long these bizarre birds have been in development down under is difficult to tell. Feathered creatures parted company with their reptilian ancestors

in Jurassic times a full 135 million years ago. But they have been evolving so fast and replacing one another with such regularity ever since then that even the most distinctively endemic of the Australian birds need not be very old inhabitants of the continent in their present form.

Since birds can fly, it follows purely on logical grounds that they have reached Australia regularly and have kept their representation there more well rounded and up-to-date than that of the mammals or reptiles.

The most archaic birds in the Australasian area are probably the kiwis of New Zealand, the cassowaries of New Guinea and Queensland, and the emus of Australia. And these, too, are thought to have come originally by flying—this despite the fact that none of them can fly today. According to current theories, they lost the power of flight after their arrival.

WHO KILLED THE MOAS?

No one knows exactly when the huge, flightless moas vanished from New Zealand, or who caused their extinction. The Maori once wore moa feathers, and their mythology tells of a "down-covered demon shaped like a bird." Yet there is a gap of about half a century between the most recent known moa bones and the arrival of Maori in 1350. It is probable that few of the birds survived an earlier society of "moa-hunters," who buried their dead with moa bones and eggs. Half the size of a 12-foot moa, a pre-Maori man is shown as he may have looked wearing a necklace made from pieces of moa thighbones and a whale's tooth pendant.

Aᴜsᴛʀᴀʟɪᴀ's one surviving species of emu stands five feet tall and weighs as much as 120 pounds. Distinctively stupid, endearingly droll, insanely inquisitive, it grazes and runs in small flocks on the great arid plains outback. With its broad stubby beak, it feeds mainly on grass but will also gourmandize on almost any food, including insects, roots, fruits, leaves and old boots. Its wide-ranging appetite, plus an ability to crash through paddock fences when running at top speed, makes it the bane of farmers and grazers, who regularly shoot it and smash its eggs in regions of the interior where it is still unprotected by game laws. In South Australia, along one 500-mile stretch of fence which stockmen have erected to keep it out of sheep pastures, it sometimes breaks through and it has been clocked on highways at up to 40 miles per hour.

During the mating season, emus team up in monogamous pairs and call to one another explosively with great booming voices. When 10 or 12 dark-green five-inch eggs have been deposited in a mat of grass, the male steps in and undertakes the whole of the nesting duties himself. This takes a full eight weeks, one of the most prolonged incubation periods known among birds. Should the female attempt to incubate the eggs, the male will drive her off.

Shorter by a head, and considerably less hefty, the cassowary stalks after fruit and berries in the tropical rain forests. In the wilds, a cassowary normally skulks out of sight in the thick of the jungle, but when flushed it makes an unforgettable impression. It runs with its head stretched forward, stoutly armed against undergrowth by a prominent "helmet." This is cushioned by light spongy bone and is believed to serve as a kind of bumper, protecting the skull against collisions with tree trunks. The body that follows is wedge-shaped and bristles with hard spiny feathers that serve to ward off vines, thorns and leaf blades. Propelled by its powerful legs, the creature can plow at remarkable speed through almost any type of vegetation: grassland, swamp or seemingly impenetrable jungle. If cornered, a cassowary will jump high and strike out to the front with its sturdy three-clawed feet. Many a Melanesian native has lost an arm or an entire stomach by chevying it too close.

New Zealand's tailless, hairy-feathered, whiskery-faced kiwi, named by the Maori for the shrill call it makes, is a far less obstreperous islander, no bigger than a rooster—although much rounder and heavier. Like the emu or cassowary, it has solid mammal-like bones and is said to be capable of running fast for short distances when pursued. For the most part, however, it struts about slowly and inconspicuously at night, high on the forested slopes of New Zealand's mountains. With rather weak sight, it intermittently touches down its long six-inch beak as if feeling its way with a cane. But the cane is not for walking.

It is tipped—uniquely among birds—with nostrils at the very end. And through these the kiwi is sniffing out the delicate aromas of earthworms and grubs.

The kiwi is the last of a whole order of New Zealand birds, the Apteryges, which once included more than 20 species of moas, some of which were giant forms strutting twice as high as a man, on leg bones as solid as those of an ox. By radiocarbon dating, moas are known to have survived at least to 1290 A.D. If the kiwi is a small aberrant offshoot of the moa, as some ornithologists believe, it reflects its heritage in the enormous eggs it lays. These are five inches long and weigh as much as a quarter of the mother bird delivering them. Per pound of mother, they are the largest eggs known. By contrast, the seven-inch ostrich egg, per pound of mother, is the smallest egg known.

The idea that moas evolved in New Zealand in response to the absence of mammals was first suggested by Charles Darwin in 1835 and is now generally accepted as true.

Possibly a slightly different explanation applies to the grass-eating emus, cassowaries, African ostriches and South American rheas, which have evolved in continental regions in the presence of mammals. All these huge running birds are primitive, and it may be that they got their start well back in the Cenozoic era, when mammals offered less by way of competition than they do today. Certainly birds have never needed much encouragement to adopt a flightless life, since on isolated predator-free islands several different groups of them have done so.

In New Zealand, at one time or another, a remarkable number of birds, stemming from different groups, have partly or completely lost the ability to fly. Remains have been found that tell of giant grounded rails, flightless geese and heavy-legged ducks. There was even an eagle, now extinct, which had comparatively short and stubby wings. Of the birds that survived until the coming of European settlers, nearly flightless forms existed among the rails, the parrots and even the most advanced bird order, the perchers.

A pullet-sized rail, known as the weka, races through the lowland forests at night, making fast ground-level attacks on crickets, mice and the eggs of other birds, and using its wings for balance only. The ranks of nearly flightless parrots include two parakeets found on outlying islets and, on the main islands, a huge nocturnal ground parrot, the hairy-faced kakapo. The kakapo was long feared extinct but has been rediscovered eking out a living in certain upland beech forests. It forages for leaves, young shoots, berries and moss. But sometimes it climbs into the lower trees, hitching its way nimbly from branch to branch by beak and talon. And sometimes it goes on hikes through the scrub, up above the treeline, to feast on juicy "snow grass" in the alpine meadows. It has been seen using its wings to cross from one tree to another in a heavy unflapping fashion more like a marsupial glider than a bird.

Having presumably had the least time to adapt themselves to life on the ground, the most astonishing of New Zealand's inept fliers are advanced perching birds. Tiny three-inch fernbirds, which seldom fly more than a few yards, hop about among the fronds of New Zealand swamps, using their stiff tails as props and poles to assist their progress. The rare, gaudily wattled crows called kokakos—not to be confused with the kakapo parrots—hop about the leaf litter or in the tall branches of a few remaining areas of remote mountain forests. They take to the air only to glide from one tree to another.

All of these perchers can fly a little. But one of the three genera of little

THE COOPERATIVE HUIAS

The huias were the "woodpeckers" of New Zealand's mountain beech forests. The sexes had differently shaped bills, used for cooperative feeding. The strong bill of the male (top) chiseled into rotting wood, exposing grubs, and the elongated, curved forceps of the female (bottom) extracted prey which her mate could not reach, deep inside the hole. Although the Maori had always prized the huias for their black-and-white tail feathers, it was the European collector of rare birds who finally dictated their wholesale slaughter. Tempted by high prices, up to one pound for each bird, the Maori hunted them to extinction. None has been seen since 1907.

New Zealand wrens may have been earth's only perching bird ever to lose the gift of flight completely. A small, running creature, it was last seen pecking out a living among the rocks of a single outlying island. Unfortunately, no one paid much attention to it until the lighthouse keeper's cat discovered the surviving population and single-pawedly reduced it to a handful of feathery specimens. These are now interred in museum drawers in London and New York, their only epitaph the tags that label them: genus, *Traversia*, monotypic; species, *lyalli;* distribution, Stephen Island; status, extinct.

On the mainland of Australia, there are no known flightless birds except the emu and cassowary. Instead, the bird population, like that of all the warmer continental areas of the world, is distinguished by a preponderance of what ornithologists call sedentary species. Sedentaries are birds that live out their lives in the same general area where they hatched. This habit is in striking contrast to that of migratory species, which take seasonal journeys according to prescribed instinctive routing, and to that of nomadic species, which wander freely, following no pattern except the one dictated by local windfalls of food, such as great upsurges of insect populations that follow rain in the interior and trees flowering. Where there are sharp seasonal contrasts in climate, as in the Northern Hemisphere, most land birds are migratory, a few sedentary and a very few nomadic. In Australia, on the other hand, as ornithologist Allen Keast has pointed out in a recent study, some 66 per cent of the land-bird species can be classed as sedentary, 26 per cent as nomadic and only 8 per cent as migratory. What is more, the tiny minority of true north-to-south migrants consists of recent colonizers of the continent or outright foreigners.

T HERE are good climatic reasons for the singularly settled habits of most of the Australian birds. The differences in temperature between north and south Australia are so small, comparatively speaking, that food is present all year and no great gain can accrue to a bird from wintering in the tropics. Moreover, the aridity of the interior offers few attractions to itinerants from abroad. The only two Asiatic land migrants that do visit the continent—two species of swift—keep, by and large, to areas where rain has brought insects.

In the Northern Hemisphere, birds perform the two great ceremonies of their year, breeding and molting, according to the seasons. They breed in the spring and molt principally in the late summer. Over much of Australia they are governed not by the heat so much as by the rainfall. Whereas Northern Hemisphere birds seem to be triggered to mate by light—the increasing day-length of spring setting off the reproductive processes—many Australian birds mate only after rain. On the tropical north coast the time most birds breed is at the onset of, or during, the summer wet season; on the temperate south coast, it comes in spring at the end of the winter wet season. On the east coast, where there is enough water throughout the year, breeding also follows the familiar routine of birds everywhere and commences in the spring. Outback from the coasts, where rain falls capriciously, the pattern of the avian year becomes a complete jumble. The apostle bird—largest of the peculiarly Australian mudlarks, which build beautifully turned nests of clay in treetops—has been known to do what would be unheard of in a Northern Hemisphere bird: to take advantage of a good wet spell and breed and molt simultaneously.

Although most Australian birds have not succeeded in penetrating westward from Australia into the Asian continent, three important groups have managed to make the jump: honey eaters, parrots and incubator birds.

The honey eaters have penetrated northeast to Hawaii, southeast to New Zealand and northwest across Wallace's line into Bali. They are small brush-tongued nectar feeders belonging to the upper echelon of perchers, the song-birds. Nearly half of the 160-odd species are exclusively Australian, and as a group they are believed to serve as the principal pollinators of the eucalypts. Although often described as sedentary, many of them actually qualify as "blossom nomads." That is, they live in restricted areas and migrate locally as one or another species of plant bursts into flower. By pursuing blossoms, some honey eaters have become long-range explorers. It may be that the species which once journeyed to Hawaii, 5,000 miles from home, simply followed favorite flowers across Polynesia, finding new favorites and forming new tastes in the sea-girt bowers along the way.

T HE 50-odd species of Australian parrots come from a considerably older bird group than any of the perchers—so old, in fact, that the world's other main parrot center is far-off South America. Fossils of parrots from Europe, dating back about 50 million years, suggest that during balmy times in the early Eocene, parrots ranged widely over the whole earth. The Australo-Papuan parrot group has spread north as far as the Philippine Islands and has responded to the environment at home with every degree of vagrancy or settledness, occupying every kind of plant community and radiating almost as widely into various niches as the marsupials.

In moving north against the predominantly southward flow of life into New Guinea and Australia, probably no native creature has succeeded better than the megapode, or incubator bird, whose eggs mature in ingenious hatcheries in the earth. Incubator birds possibly originated in the New Guinea region, although the three most diverse forms today are Australian. They have infiltrated across Wallace's line as far west as the Andamans and north to the Philippines, and penetrated Micronesia as far north as the Marianas.

Incubator birds come of very early fowl, pheasant and turkey stock. Moreover they bury their eggs in the primeval manner of reptiles. But the care and hatching of these buried eggs involve one of the most sophisticated and highly evolved patterns of bird behavior known. In their New Guinea homelands the incubator birds erect enormous mounds of plant debris as much as 35 feet in diameter and 15 feet high. In these they lay their eggs and then rely on heat from the fermenting compost to insure a healthy hatching.

To the north and south of New Guinea, incubator birds have harnessed several other unusual sources of heat to do their hatching for them. In north Celebes they come down out of mountain hideaways for two months out of every year, take over certain stretches of black beach and lay their large four-inch eggs in holes for the sun to hatch, taking advantage of the fact that black sand soaks up more heat from the sun than white sand. Some Celebes megapodes dispense with the annual pilgrimage to the coast and bury their eggs, right where they live, in what seems to be cold mountain clay. Ornithologists were mystified by these apparent attempts at infanticide until they discovered that the eggs in the hills were invariably planted close to hot springs, where they would be warmed by heat from the subterranean regions of the earth.

To the south in Australia, as the climate becomes more temperate with increasing latitude, buried eggs prove ever more troublesome for adult incubator birds to keep at the right temperature. Yet one genus of incubator bird, the mallee fowl, manages to survive across almost all of the southern half of the

MOUND-DWELLING PARROT

Although most parrots nest in hollow trees, five or six species in Australia and New Guinea have learned to dig into termite mounds and hollow out a nesting chamber inside. Shown here is a male paradise parrot, next to the entrance tunnel it has made, and a female (in cutaway) incubating her eggs. The nest is lined with papery debris from termite tunnels. The insects in the mound do not bother the birds; they bring clay from the surrounding soil, and seal themselves off from their boarders to keep their own nurseries and eggs from drying out.

WOOD-PECKING PARROT

Woodpeckers do not occur in Australia, but the niche that they occupy on other continents is filled down under by a few species of cockatoos with strong hooked bills, which are used for cracking seeds, and also for digging wood-boring grubs out of the trees. The aggressive yellow-tailed cockatoo, shown here, strips off Eucalyptus bark and gouges out holes eight or more inches deep in rotted wood to extract the larvae of beetles. Its thorough foraging, especially in old, decayed trunks and branches, helps to keep many of the timber-destroying pests in check.

continent, living wherever there is dry eucalypt scrub or mallee. In these regions the temperature of the air may drop by as much as 30° between noon and midnight, and there is not enough water in the ground during the summer to make fermentation of compost a completely dependable source of heat.

Nobody suspected the fantastically complex pattern of behavior involved in the hatching of mallee fowl eggs until Australian biologist H. J. Frith carried out researches into the biology of the species in recent years. It was found that breeding activities occupy its energies for no less than 11 months out of every year. Starting about April, after the first autumnal shower of the winter wet season, a typical pair of mallee fowl works together to dig a wide hole two to three feet deep, in which it lays down a compost bed of wet twigs and leaves. By the time the winter has reached its peak, this rubbish has begun to rot and the provident pair heaps up to two or three feet of sand over it to seal in the moisture and the heat of decomposition. In the heart of the finished mound, surrounded by warm compost, is the egg chamber, a pocket of finely divided leaves and sand. At about this stage in the work, the male takes charge and leaves the female free to rest and fatten up for the egg laying ahead. She begins to lay early in spring and continues, an egg at a time, at two-to-17-day intervals, for the next five or six months.

Throughout the laying period the male sleeps near the mound, feeds near the mound and works on it literally day and night. His task is to keep the egg chamber inside at a constant temperature of from 90° to 96° Fahrenheit. He performs it so zealously that if the female comes around to lay an egg at the wrong time—when opening the incubator might let in too much hot sun or cold rain water—he chases her away and lets her drop her egg where she may.

Apparently the male mallee fowl is able to judge the temperature in the incubator by means of his beak, which he periodically plunges into the mound with all the authority of a registered nurse wielding a thermometer. Having measured the temperature, he must then regulate it, and this requires different action at different times. In spring, when the first eggs are laid, heat from the dank compost underground is rapidly percolating upward and tends to reach dangerous peaks during the warmth of the day. The male mallee fowl prepares for overheating by opening up the mound in the small hours of the night, spreading out the layers of sand and then feverishly piling them back onto the mound when they have been well chilled by the early morning air. As the dry summer progresses, the compost loses moisture, ferments more slowly and produces less heat. The heat of the noonday sun, however, becomes so intense that the driven male, in addition to uncovering the incubator during the night, must now also work to cover it up again with an increasingly thick layer of insulation.

As autumn approaches, matters improve· for a while and then deteriorate rapidly. Fermentation ceases altogether and the nights turn cold. The zealous male works with rising desperation to try to maintain the proper temperature, opening the nest to the sun at midday and heaping it high with hot sand before evening. Finally, however, the temperature in the incubator drops hopelessly, the male gives up the struggle, and for about a month he and his mate wander away from the mound and enjoy a brief vacation before starting on their next year's chores. Mallee fowl may never see any of their chicks. When an egg hatches in the incubator, seven weeks or more after it is laid, the young one laboriously digs its way to the surface. It may take as much as 17 hours to emerge, but an hour later it can run fairly well, and in 24 hours it can fly. From the moment it awakes underground, it is entirely on its own.

The obsessive zeal of the male mallee fowl is an extreme example of male responsibility among those birds that have only one mate in a breeding season or for life. Most such birds share the responsibilities of egg care with the females. This condition is so widespread that some students of birds believe it is primitive and has characterized bird behavior almost from the beginning. On the other hand, among the archaic cassowaries and emus, all the egg-guarding and fledgling-feeding is undertaken by the males. The male kiwi will sit for as much as 80 days on one egg and may not leave it to feed for a week at a time.

Periodically in the course of bird evolution an altogether different type of mating behavior has cropped up in which the male takes no part in incubation, usually practices promiscuous mating and often displays his genetic virtues to the opposite sex through gaudy plumage, fancy dancing or melodious singing. Bird-filled Australasia provides extraordinary examples of male display in the lyrebirds, the birds of paradise and the bowerbirds.

In the music it makes, the Australian lyrebird proves itself one of the most accomplished of all perching birds. It happens also to be the largest, about three and one half feet in length. Apart from its own variable, bubbling, beautiful songs, it mocks perfectly the voices it hears. It mimics the gay laughter of the kookaburra, or "laughing jackass," as readily as the singing of a thrush. Its imitations include the liquid notes of the golden whistler, the screeching of cockatoos, the warbles of butcherbirds, plus the sounds made by scrub wrens, pilot birds, owls, whipbirds, tree creepers, even industrial machinery and auto horns. When taken to a new land, it quickly picks up the songs of the native birds without forfeiting those of its compatriots at home. On one occasion, a group of lumbermen were reported to have stopped work because a lyrebird mocked the local mill whistle.

The lyrebird's song is closely tied in with other courtship activities. That is, it dances while it sings and does both routines on a set stage in the forest where the female can come and look it over during its entertainment. In repose, it is not obviously a showy bird except that it has a fine, long tail. When opened up, this tail is revealed as an exquisitely lacy fan, spread between a pair of curving outer plumes.

During display, the male lyrebird raises its fan up and over its back until the plumes begin to hang in front of its head. Since the feathers are brown on top and silvery white on the underside, the display at zenith turns the lyrebird from a drab denizen of dark forests into a brilliant cascade of silver. Slowly the silver droplets surround the bird's head. As it moves about its dance mound they shiver and shimmer, vibrating delicately with the exertions of its singing.

WHAT is the function of this breathtakingly beautiful performance? Nobody knows, although some observers, noting that the male display grounds are widely spaced, believe that the activity of the males is a device for luring females to the mounds so that mating can be achieved without fighting between males. Emphasis is given this view by there being only one nest per territory and by the fact that the species is thought to be monogamous for the duration of the breeding season. Whichever the case, once mating takes place, the female builds her nest and incubates her eggs alone. The male goes on tending his stage and singing and dancing the season through.

Of polygamous birds that display in certain well-defined areas, none are more spectacular than the birds of paradise of the New Guinea region. Only peacocks can vie with birds of paradise for sheer dazzling beauty. Though near relatives of the smart, unhandsome crows, they waft head crests, tail plumes, breast shields, beards, bibs and tuckers that cannot be rivaled in either shape or color. Most major mountaintops in New Guinea are ecological islands and hide their own distinctive forms and wondrous spectacle of displaying birds. Some of the paradise birds hang upside down in their displays, some clip foliage to let shafts of light filter through layers of jungle vegetation onto their display courts, some dance in the treetops, some in clearings expressly made for the purpose on the forest floor. Among certain species of displaying birds, according to ornithologist Thomas Gilliard, a group of males maintains an "arena" in the forest, set aside solely for display and courting. Within the arena each male has its own private clearing. There seem to be certain preferred areas—perhaps in the center—that are the most attractive to the females. Thus, there is a great deal of competition for these preferred sites before each male bird settles down on its own property. The contests themselves involve singing and plumage display. It is now believed that these displays function as a means both of establishing breeding rights among males and of attracting the females. Through their exquisite displays, the finest of the male paradise birds may mate with many females in a season, while less handsome ones, who own peripheral territories, may not father so much as a single egg. As a result the characteristics of relatively few males are passed on to succeeding generations and the rate of evolution is accelerated.

A NOVEL departure in this pattern of exaggerated male display behavior—one that in Gilliard's view may represent a "breakthrough" in bird evolution—has been developed in the New Guinea and Australian region by a group of bird of paradise relatives, the bowerbirds. Instead of showing off their own sexual plumage in a flashy way that might attract predators, some bowerbirds have transferred their display instincts to inanimate objects. The males construct elaborate tunnel- or wigwam-shaped bachelor apartments from bits of ground cover interwoven with twigs. They adorn these bowers with highly colorful heaps of feathers, pebbles, shells and fruits. If opportunity offers, they add aluminum camping spoons, shards of broken pop bottles, silver coins or any other bauble they can find, including, on one occasion, a glass eye. Some of them plant the display clearings around their quarters with carefully tended lawns of soft growing moss. Some of them chew up charcoal or berries to make pigments which they apply to the walls with paint brushes of chewed-up leaves or bark. The females often watch these building operations as attentively as other arena females watch a full-scale display of gorgeous plumage. If satisfied with the furnishings, a bowerbird female enters the bower and copulation occurs.

The agriculture of the male bowerbird in getting moss to grow is without parallel among birds. His use of artifacts—of ornaments and paint brushes—is unique. There are other extraordinary feathered entrepreneurs, however—such as the incubator birds, which exploit volcanoes; the butcherbirds, which impale victims on thorns for storage; and the buzzard, which is said to take up stones to break open emu eggs. Some ornithologists believe that bowerbirds may stand at the apex of avian evolution. And though not all agree, the attainments of the bowerbirds, and of the lyre and paradise birds as well, suggest that at least some bird evolution in Australasia has proceeded further than mammal, reptile or frog evolution. The winged ones, in short, have done well down under.

LARGEST AND SHOWIEST OF ITS GROUP, THE RAINBOW LORIKEET SUPPLEMENTS A LIQUID DIET OF NECTAR WITH SEEDS FROM A "GRASS TREE"

A Bird Paradise

More varied than any other vertebrate group in Australasia, birds are represented by 58 families, a fifth of them endemic, ranging from the most primitive (flightless kiwis and mound-building megapodes) to the most advanced (exotic birds of paradise and bowerbirds). More than 50 kinds of parrots and such improbable birds as the black swan and kookaburra live only down under.

THE PLAINS COME ALIVE AS LITTLE CORELLAS, THE MOST COMMON WHITE COCKATOOS IN THE NORTHWEST, RISE FROM THEIR EARLY MOR

SCARLET-CHESTED PARROT

RED-WINGED PARROT

The Parrot Explosion

Radiating into every corner of Australia, the parrots have developed a wide variety of feeding habits similar to those of entirely different birds and even mammals on other continents. There is only one nectar-sipping sunbird and no hummingbirds in Australia; instead, in addition to honey eaters, there are nectar-sipping lorikeets that drift from grove to grove and region to region, helping pollinate trees as they come into bloom, just as bees do. There is also a dearth of seed-eating sparrows and finches in Australia, but an abundance of large

SHY AND ELUSIVE, the forest kaka is a close relative of the kea, but eats a conventional diet of grubs, nectar, fruit and seeds—never sheep.

LURED BY A CARROT, a kea walks into a fine wire noose attached to a stick, as a trapper prepares to pull it tight. Most keas are very friendly birds, remarkably unafraid of people.

A Parrot Learns to Kill

The kea of South Island is one of the few New Zealand birds that has profited from European settlement. From the mountaintops on which it lives, this adaptable parrot has invaded the lowlands and exploited a new source of food: the carcasses of sheep. From carrion-feeding it was only a step to predatory habits. A few individuals learned to tear flesh from sheep which were weak, sick or helplessly snowed in; then they began to attack healthy sheep. Only one or two birds in a flock became killers, but the others flew in to share the carcass. Neither trapping nor shooting has discouraged the keas. Ranchers have found the best means of control is less wasteful management of their sheep; wherever the meadows are kept free of carrion, keas do not develop carnivorous habits. A close relative, the kaka, never became a meat eater. Dependent on trees for nesting hollows and food, it is gradually vanishing as timber cutting destroys its forest habitat.

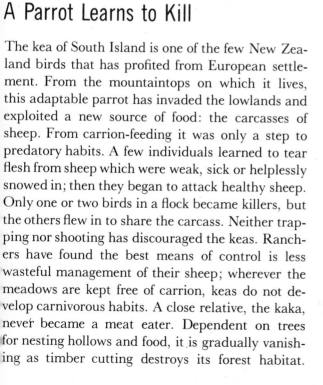

FREED FROM THE SNARE, now lying on the rocks (right), the bird allows brick-red wing linings to be displayed. Used as a decoy, it will lure other keas within shooting distance.

THE EMPRESS OF GERMANY belongs to the bird of paradise group discovered by Magellan, one of which, the greater bird of paradise, was introduced some 60 years ago to Little Tobago in the West Indies, where 35 individuals still live.

The Regal Birds of Paradise

From their first voyage around the globe, Magellan's crew returned to Europe in 1522 with two specimens of the greater bird of paradise. Unaware that native hunters had cut off the legs, 16th Century sages surmised that these were not real birds, but legless "wanderers from heaven," a superstition encouraged by their ethereal, lacy plumes, sweeping fully two feet downward from the sides of their bodies. Some 43 species have since been discovered in the New Guinea area, many so splendidly ornamented that they were originally named after European kings and queens, in the hope of securing favors or patronage. Only the males wear the regal plumes, the long whiplike tail feathers, fans, chest shields and capes.

Ironically, the ornaments which have helped them to breed and radiate successfully in the past nearly caused their extermination in recent times. Native tribesmen in the central highlands have always made towering headdresses of their plumes. With the advent of the European fad for feathered hats, entire villages became trading centers; as many as 50,000 plumed pelts were sent to Amsterdam and Paris annually. At the peak of trading, they were worth $50 apiece. By 1921, when the killing was officially stopped, many species had become more common in millinery shops than in their native forests.

THE LITTLE KING, surpassing larger birds of paradise in gem-like coloring, is their legendary monarch. It has wiry tail feathers, tightly coiled at the ends to form medallions, and green-fringed chest fans also open during display. By calling and performing antics on the branch of a tree—its "dance platform"—the male attracts a succession of temporary mates.

A MALE EMU GUARDS ITS NEST. RANCHERS SMASH EMU EGGS OR SELL THEM AS SOUVENIRS, GAILY PAINTED WITH SCENES OF AUSTRALIA

The Flightless

Three large flightless birds still survive in Australasia, each coping with man in its own way. Timid New Zealand kiwis stay hidden in underground burrows, emerging only at night to feed, and are threatened mainly by forest-clearing and introduced predators. Bold cassowaries, deep in the rain forests of New Guinea and Northern Australia, bear knifelike claws capable of delivering mortal slashes. Nevertheless, many are captured and kept in cages by New Guinea natives, who use their body plumes as currency. On dry outback plains, where the emu has come in conflict with grazers and farmers, its main defense has been to run away at speeds up to 40 miles an hour. During the "Great Emu War" of 1932, Government machine gunners were notably unsuccessful, but ranchers shoot thousands of emus for bounty each year and poison many more.

THE KIWI, last surviving relative of the moas of New Zealand, was once killed for its hairlike feathers, used in trout flies. Protected since 1921, it is New Zealand's unofficial symbol.

163

ONY HELMET AND PINK WATTLES ARE DISPLAYED BY THE JUNGLE-DWELLING AUSTRALIAN CASSOWARY

A Carefree Singer and a Careworn Builder

In Australia some male birds work much harder than others in family raising. The lyrebird does nothing but sing and dance for a short season, devoting all his energies to attracting a mate. This he does with great style (*bottom of page*), but when the dance is consummated, his responsibility is ended.

Not so the male mallee fowl. He has the principal responsibility for regulating temperature in a mound of sand and compost in which the female lays her eggs. This task occupies the hard-working fowl almost the year through, as he struggles to maintain an even 90 to 96° inside the mound by piling

THE HATCHING OF A MALLEE FOWL

AN EGG IS LAID by the mallee fowl, who croons with her mate before depositing it in the mound made of sand and vegetation. She may lay three times her weight in eggs in a year.

THE MOUND IS CLOSED by the male, who scratches sand over the eggs. Every few days the mound is reopened for another egg until the clutch—usually no more than 12—is complete.

THE COURTSHIP OF THE LYREBIRD

STARTING ITS DISPLAY, a lyrebird shows off his voice and two-foot tail on a "stage" of soil raked from the forest floor. About 75 per cent of his repertoire is mimicry of other birds.

AT THE PEAK OF DISPLAY, the tail plumes are thrown over the bird's head. He sometimes pirouettes and jumps for as long as half an hour, and may repeat his dance six times a day.

up or taking away soil. His efforts have been studied by the biologist H. J. Frith, who inserted thermometers in mounds and demonstrated that the mallee fowl's activities did indeed regulate mound temperature, encouraging heat from compost fermentation early in the season and preventing excess heat from the sun later on. Frith also counted the visits to the mounds by placing taut cords in the mounds and attaching them to recording devices. These were agitated by the fowls while digging. Some of the birds he watched worked so hard during the hot season that they were literally panting with exhaustion.

TESTING THE TEMPERATURE in the mound, the male uses his partly opened bill. Sand is added or removed according to the "reading" taken by the heat-sensitive bill and tongue.

A CHICK EMERGES after prolonged digging. It takes seven to nine weeks to hatch, but is well developed and quickly becomes self-sufficient. It can run in an hour, fly the next day.

ATTRACTED BY THE DANCE, a female approaches and is enveloped by tail feathers just before mating. She has already started to build a nest some distance from the display area.

THE BREEDING SEASON OVER, the male sheds his plumes. During the 10 weeks of growing in new ones, he is a drab, quiet bird, preoccupied with scratching in the soil for worms.

A FLOATING NEST of sticks, reeds and rushes is home for a pair of marsh-dwelling black swans. In it they will raise as many as eight or nine fluffy chicks. Pairs often gather together and live in groups in Australia's coastal rivers and lakes. In recent years black swans have been introduced into New Zealand, Europe and America, where they now breed in parks.

A ROCKHOPPER cradles its egg. Killed in the 1920s as a source of oil, the rockhoppers were nearly wiped out. Then the shooting ceased and their breeding grounds became crowded again.

The Eccentrics

Among Australasia's most unusual inhabitants are the world's only black swan, a kingfisher that has forgotten how to fish, and the rockhopper, a crested penguin. Until the Dutch navigator De Vlamingh sighted black swans on the southwest coast of Australia in 1679, it was axiomatic in Europe that "all swans are white." The discovery of black ones down under established the continent's reputation as a land of paradox.

The kookaburra is famous for its habit of getting together with other kookaburras and filling the air with loud, cackling laughter. The largest of the kingfishers, it has developed a taste for reptiles and rodents—and for this is so highly regarded by farmers that it has been introduced into Western Australia and Tasmania. Visitors from the southern ocean, rockhoppers come ashore only to breed by the hundreds of thousands on the subantarctic islands. There they present a fantastic spectacle—hopping in the rocks with yellow and black plumes flopping.

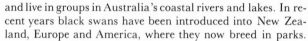

THE KOOKABURRA, although it is a predator, has weak feet and a straight bill, and cannot rip its prey apart as hawks do. Instead, it gradually worries it into a pulp or into small pieces.

8

Human Holdovers

from the

Stone Age

O F the countless forms of life which have found sanctuary in Australia and
gained a respite from extinction, the last to arrive was Stone Age man.
He came not tens of millions of years ago, like the marsupials or the emus, but
perhaps only 20 or 30 thousand years ago. Yet such is the pace of man's cultural evolution, as distinct from the purely biological evolution of animals, that
the Australian aborigines have proved more defenseless against competition
from outside than the hoary tuatara, the platypus, the koala or the kiwi. In less
than 200 years of European settlement, the Tasmanian natives have died out
completely and the mainland aborigines have been diminished and transformed.
Out of an original population estimated at 300,000, only 41,000 full bloods remain. Of these, about 1,000 wander in the virgin wastelands of the west and
still practice the Stone Age arts of their ancestors. Another 12,000 are gainfully
employed in mines or on cattle and sheep stations, and may ultimately make
the wrenching leap into modern society. Only 2,000 already live in cities. The
remaining 26,000—among them the aged and the recently "detribalized"—live
on mission stations or in government reserves, where they are being gradually
exposed to the white man's way of life.

This appalling decline of the entire Australoid race—one of the four or five races, or subspecies, usually recognized by anthropologists—has not come about because of any concerted genocide on the part of the white Australians. To be sure, aborigines were sometimes treated like animals and even hunted or poisoned like animals in the early days of settlement, but there were no organized killings comparable to the Indian wars in the United States or the Maori wars in New Zealand. Instead the aborigines have succumbed to Western diseases, have produced relatively few children and have died, as it were, out of sheer demoralization. Their way of life depends not only on complex and vivid religious practices, but on the preservation of tribal ancestral hunting grounds. Loss of either (and they are losing both) destroys their will to live.

Before the coming of Europeans, the 300,000 aborigines occupied the whole vast three million square miles of Australia. No other continent, except, of course, Antarctica, was so sparsely populated. But then again, no other in historic times was settled exclusively by Old or Middle Stone Agers— by men innocent not only of all metalworking, but of all agriculture and husbandry as well. Under the hand of the aborigines, the scant bounty of the wilds was never improved by stocking with flocks or crops, and the number of inhabitants an area could support was infinitesimal compared to its potential under even the crudest forms of farming or herding. In lean years aboriginal men automatically regulated their numbers by disgruntled fighting; women, having no domestic milk animals, sometimes had to kill newborn infants if they still had older babies at the breast and their own milk supply began to run low.

The studies of anthropologists suggest that the aboriginal population of pre-colonial Australia may have stood near the 300,000 mark for thousands of years; that it may have reached this level and risen no higher because simple food-gathering techniques, in the niggardly Eden of much of the Australian environment, would support no more souls. Each of some 700 aboriginal tribes, consisting of roughly 400 to 500 individuals apiece, had its own tribal territory. In most areas, the boundaries of each territory were well established and considered rigid and ancient by the tribesmen concerned. Moreover, the size of each territory corresponded well with the amount of food to be found on it. Along the verdant east coast, a tribe of 500 might claim no more than 150 square miles of land. On the arid plains, by comparison, a tribe of the same size might wander over as much as 40,000 square miles. To each individual of either group would fall roughly the same portion of food, but in collecting it, the easterner might have to shift camp only three or four times a year, while the desert dweller might have to sleep annually by a hundred different campsites and travel on foot over 1,000 miles.

So close to his native earth was the aboriginal that every boy on the desert had to memorize the exact location and names of all springs, mudholes and water-collecting crannies within his people's domain. So widely known were the tribal frontiers that they have a peculiar way of coinciding on the map with routes of early explorers—the point being that native guides, though often far from their own home districts, took care to keep their white charges from trespassing on ancient prerogatives. Except on special prearranged occasions, such as the delivery of a bride or the journey to a great festive gathering of the clans, a man seldom left his home range without risking a fight. A woman, on the other hand, often left forever when she was taken to live in the camp of her husband. He was generally a man chosen for her by one of her elder kinsmen

—commonly her mother's brother—in a parley with her future father-in-law. Sometimes the arrangement had been made, on the assumption that she would be a girl, even before her birth.

The aborigines have obviously evolved their close relationship with the soils, plants and animals of Australia over many generations. When and how they first came to Australia are questions on which anthropologists do not agree. The most concerted effort to find answers, however, and to offer a comprehensive theory of the aborigines has been made by the Australian anthropologist Norman B. Tindale and the American anthropologist Joseph B. Birdsell. It is their theory which is described in the pages that follow.

According to the deductions of Tindale and Birdsell, the first aborigines established themselves in Australia between 18,000 and 30,000 years ago. At about this time, the last ice age, which reached its zenith approximately 25,000 years ago, was pushing all sorts and conditions of men out of the melting pot of Asia down into the tropical Malayan region. Clans backward in Stone Age technology were crowded toward extinction. Some held out in mountain strongholds or forest fastnesses, where a few endure even today. Others, forced into beachcombing and hazardous reef-fishing on Stone Age rafts, gradually trickled across straits of open water to the dim island outlines on the horizon. Driven as much by wind and accident as by intention, they reached the Andamans, Japan, the Philippines, Borneo and Celebes, the Sundas and Moluccas, New Guinea and ultimately Australia.

At the time, so much of the world's water was locked up solid as snow and ice on the land that the oceans lay depleted, some 250 feet lower than at present. Wide margins along the present continental shelves emerged as terra firma. New Guinea, Tasmania and some of the Melanesian islands were connected to Australia by broad isthmuses. In the northwest, Java, Sumatra and Borneo were part of continental Asia. Between the two amplified land masses, islands and reefs reared so high that the broadest straits are estimated to have been no more than 20 or 30 miles wide, as compared with 100 miles today. On a clear day a harried Stone Ager could probably always see from the beach of one steppingstone the hazy hope of another across the water.

RELENTLESSLY the underdogs of one millennium were followed by those of the next: the hairy white Ainu of Hokkaido by the first Japanese; the Negrito of Luzon by the Igorot, Ilokano and Tagalog; the Negritoid hill folk of New Guinea by so many waves of whitish, brownish and yellowish people that the terms "Papuan," "Melanesian" and "Polynesian" today signify stews of inextricably complex racial ingredients.

The earliest waves of these many migrations, on reaching New Guinea, spread across the land bridge into Australia. Then, after the last ice age came to an end about 10,000 years ago, the seas gradually rose, and by 4700 B.C. Australia was once more cut off. Until the arrival of the convicts at Botany Bay in 1788, there were probably no more major influxes of human beings, only cultural influxes generated by seafarers and castaways—by Melanesians, Malaysians and perhaps Polynesians touching on the northern coast.

The Australoids, who had walked over from New Guinea in the days of low ocean, are sometimes considered a single, rather primitive race, characterized by their beetling brows and sprawling, bridgeless noses. Tindale and Birdsell, however, have distinguished three separate and probably successive types of aborigines: an early wave of diminutive brown Negritos, a later wave of light-

THE VERSATILE BOOMERANG

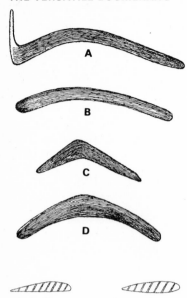

The boomerang that the aboriginal uses for hunting (B) is fairly straight and streamlined in cross section (F). It is thrown directly at game and does not return. A picklike tip may be added (A) to make a more lethal fighting weapon. Returning boomerangs (C, D) are lighter, have an airfoil shape (E) and are used as toys and in sporting contests.

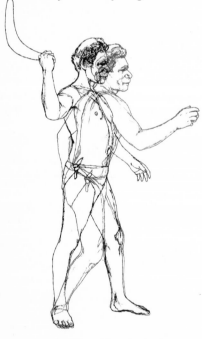

To throw a returning boomerang, the aboriginal grasps an end, keeping the curved upper surface facing his body. He throws overhand, adding a sharp flick of the wrist as he lets go. He must aim into the wind to make a boomerang come back.

skinned Australoids and a final wave of darker Australoids. European settlers found the most pronouncedly Negritoid aborigines living in the land's-end outpost of Tasmania. Though none of them now remain to be studied except a few mixed bloods, they are thought by Birdsell and Tindale to have been a hybrid race compounded of early pygmy Negritoids and later true Australoids. An almost pure group of some 600 pygmy Negritoids survives around mission stations in and near the largest tropical rain-forest area of northern Queensland. They are similar to other relict Negritoid groups holding out as agile tree climbers in deeply forested enclaves on the Andaman Islands, Palawan and Luzon in the Philippines, and upland areas of New Guinea, Bougainville and the New Hebrides.

THE true Australoids, in the Tindale-Birdsell view, followed the Negritoids into Australia and largely replaced them. First came the "Murrayians," typified by the aborigines which survived in the Murray Basin and on the east, south and west coasts at the time of European settlement. Later the Murrayians were succeeded throughout the northern and central regions of the continent by more advanced Australoids, which Tindale and Birdsell have named "Carpentarians" after the Gulf of Carpentaria in the north. Because of the regions they inhabited, the Murrayian aborigines have been disbanded and dispossessed by white settlement. Enough of them remain as individuals, however, to make Tindale and Birdsell think that they were a thickset, hirsute people of light-brown complexion, somewhat resembling the Ainu of Japan. At birth many of the southern aborigines were so fair-skinned and towheaded that their mothers rubbed them down with emu grease to serve as suntan lotion. Today the survivors, when not exposed much to the sun, retain pale skin even as adults. The long, brown hair of the Murrayians, instead of crinkling or crisping like the locks of the Tasmanians, merely curled gently.

The third wave of aboriginal Australians recognized by Birdsell and Tindale was built along typically Australoid lines so far as bone and skull structure were concerned, but its representatives had brown and rather hairless skin, like many of the Melanesians and Malaysians to the north. They also possessed an arsenal of refined stone and wooden implements, and at the coming of the whites, they had spread widely, populating the entire northern and most of the central regions of the continent.

Birdsell and Tindale roughly identify the Tasmanian Negritoid and earlier and later Australoid elements in the aboriginal population with successive archeological levels in Stone Age culture. The first culture, the Kartan, was probably associated with the Negritoids. It prevailed from about 26,000 to 10,000 years ago. It was distinguished by digging sticks, round river stones flaked on one side for use as hand axes, wooden spears to be thrown by hand, and sharp shells for use in scraping fish and cutting hides. In a later phase of cultural development, called the Tartangan, the Negritoids improved slightly on all these tools and left in their campsites occasional bone fragments of the ice-age *Diprotodon* and giant emus. Tartangan culture continued on in some parts of the mainland until a mere 6,000 years ago—until not long before the pharaohs began constructing pyramids. In a few places in Western Australia, aborigines were still wielding implements similar to Tartangan ones when first discovered by white settlers.

The next advances up the cultural ladder—advances which Birdsell and Tindale associate with the Murrayians—brought barbed wooden spearheads, sharp flaked-off stone dagger blades, and possibly boomerangs and woomeras into the Paleolithic armory. The woomera is a spear thrower, a stick with a wooden pin lashed to one end of it with sinews. The pin fits into the butt of the spear and conveys thrust to it. When skillfully used, the woomera levers a spear into its trajectory with far greater force—far more deadly thrust and accuracy—than an unaided hand can.

The boomerang, as we usually think of it, is a flat crescent-shaped stick which whirls through the air in a spiraling arc that sweeps back toward the thrower. The aborigines' everyday weapon, however, was a heavy nonreturning boomerang which could be either thrown or wielded as a sword. Similar throwing sticks have been hurled by many primitive peoples, including American Indians and ancient Egyptians, and their remains have even been found in Danish peat bogs. Because they revolve as they fly, their tips travel at enormous speed and pack considerably more wallop on impact than a nonspinning missile such as a thrown rock.

The lighter-weight returning boomerang was exclusively an Australoid invention and represented an elegant refinement on the art of stick-throwing. Though used mainly in games and tournaments, or for amusing children, it played an important part in at least one serious activity: the duck hunt. Crouching beside an oxbow lake in one of the half-dry river courses, a duck hunter would hurl his boomerang above a flight of oncoming birds. At the same time he would screech like a duck hawk. Tricked by his calls and by the shadow of the boomerang overhead, the ducks would dive low into nets staked out or held up by collaborating hunters farther down the billabong. Instead of falling into the water, the boomerang, meanwhile, would land at the feet of the thrower and be ready at hand for the next flight of ducks and the next cast.

THE final stage in aboriginal technology is associated by Birdsell and Tindale with the tall, willowy, smooth-skinned, dark-brown Carpentarians, who survive little trammeled today along the north coast and down into the central deserts. Carpentarians knit bags out of palm-tassel string; model with bee's wax; paint pictures on cave walls or bark; haft their spears, wherever possible, with straight featherweight bamboo; sharpen their axe heads by a crude form of grinding; and on the seacoast, fashion two-ended canoes instead of mere bark saucers like the Murrayians. Some of them even have acquired the Malaysian arts of shaping dugout canoes and using sails made of pandanus leaves.

So much for the Tindale-Birdsell view—condensed here for purposes of clarity. It is persuasive in that it makes a good attempt to reconcile a great deal of shadowy, often confused and sometimes even contradictory information. However, it is by no means the only view. Other anthropologists believe that the aborigines constitute a single geographical race of extreme variability in its physical characteristics. This variability expressed itself genetically during long periods of isolation in Australia by different groups of people. To unravel the story today, complicated as it is by subsequent mixings of these groups and by continued invasions from the Asiatic mainland, is almost impossible.

But whatever the truth may be, most experts are agreed that during one of the later stages of prehistoric culture, the aborigines were joined by the dingo, a half-domesticated dog akin to the Indian wolf. The earliest dingo remains probably go back to about 6,000 years ago, but the most surely dated ones were left only about 3,000 years ago. It is in the short span since one or another of these limits that the dingo has run wild, possibly being responsible for

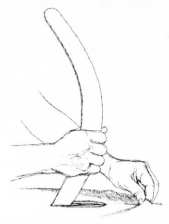

The boomerang is used for many purposes. Its sharp edge makes an efficient knife for cutting up and skinning kangaroos and emus. It is plunged into the soft skin of the underbelly and pulled back sharply to make a long, clean cut.

Two boomerangs clapped together provide a rhythmic background for many aboriginal dances. One Central Australian boomerang has sharp fluted ridges so that when one is drawn across the other like a bow, a musical tone is produced.

Used as a trowel or digging stick, the boomerang enables a man to dig a cooking pit, open up a well or ferret out a burrowing animal. Boomerangs are also used to retouch stone blades, to start fires, and as swords and clubs in combat.

exterminating the pouched wolf and Tasmanian devil from the Australian mainland, and causing unknown decimations in the rest of the marsupial population. Stone Age man himself, with his firestick, has probably brought about significant changes in the Australian environment. Patches of savanna in the northeastern rain forests and groups of fire-resistant trees along his paths in savanna woodlands have been ascribed to his ancient habit of torching dry areas to drive out small game from the underbrush. Possibly, too, the extinction of the *Diprotodon* and giant ice-age kangaroos and emus can be laid at his door.

COMMUNICATION WITHOUT WORDS

Although they have no written language, the aborigines have developed several effective ways of communicating with each other without talking. Hand signals (below) may have helped bridge the language barrier between tribes, since there are nearly 500 dialects spoken in Australia. But their principal purpose is to communicate silently while hunting, or during ceremonies when speech is taboo. Old women use hand signals as needing less effort than speech.

WHO ARE YOU?

POSSUM

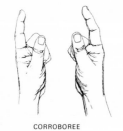

CORROBOREE

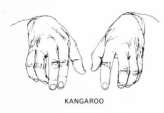

KANGAROO

Hand signs, called ideagrams, may express an abstract phrase such as "Who are you?" or something visible like claw marks on a tree: the sign for "possum." Signs also convey words by describing actions: the clapping of invisible boomerangs to suggest a corroboree or the curled forepaws of a hopping kangaroo.

THE extent of the balance that the aborigines were able to maintain with their environment offers modern science an unparalleled opportunity to understand the niche in nature occupied by the human species only a few thousand years ago, before it began to reshape the floras and faunas of the earth with agriculture, grazing and suburban sprawl. All the aborigines' fine animal attunements to nature which have been noticed by scientists and swagmen fill books of description. An impression of them can perhaps be gleaned from the following diary of a day, drawn from research made by Tindale for a film and written as it might be jotted down by a young anthropologist on the march with a group of desert tribesmen.

"Awake at the first hint of daylight. Slight frost on the ground. Have been shivering all night in spite of fires they kindly lit on both sides of me. You have to roll over every 15 minutes and jam together the stick ends in those fires if you want to stay half alive. Scholander has shown that aborigines sleep without shivering under these conditions because their blood vessels help them arrive at a state of 'depth insulation.' Capillary networks between arteries and veins leading to skin exchange heat. The blood returning to the heart arrives without any shocking chill in it and the blood going to the extremities carries no unnecessary warmth. The feet of the naked aboriginal may cool to 54° F., while his heart remains warm. The lucky fellow must stir less often than a white man to stoke those wretched fires. Even so, he sleeps fitfully, often lying next to a dog for warmth. He will also nap during the day to make up for sleep lost at night.

"The woman on the next plot of ground is asking her toddler about the pygmy imprints of a spider left in the night across a bit of sand beside them. Baby knows who spider is and which way he was going.

"Other women are returning from water hole with deep boat-shaped wooden dishes full of water for breakfast. We ate all the available solid food last night. As men stir and quench thirsts, women pack digging sticks and shallow scooping and winnowing plates of bark or wood into their big boat-shaped wooden dishes for carrying on heads. They know that unless they are ready, men will growl, strike or simply move out for march unencumbered by anything but spears and woomeras. Studies have shown that the men set a high value on their freedom to pick up and walk whenever they want to. Paleolithic tools worth carrying are many-purpose and light of weight. All other tools are made and discarded in the same day or cached by a water hole for future use.

"In addition to sticks and plates, women also contrive to carry smoldering faggots, the raw materials for next campfire. If rain puts out fire or firesticks, any of men can usually make more by friction methods. But in case of a drenching downpour, all tinder may be soaked and someone may have to walk dozens of miles to borrow a light from the next nearest clan. This is known to have happened and the price may run high, not only for the chilly stay-at-home but also for the Promethean fire-seekers venturing into alien country.

"As party sets off, young men fan out on either side of vanguard. This is heartening. It means we have to walk 10 miles at the utmost. If the next water were more than 10 miles away, the hunters would walk straight ahead purposefully at least throughout the morning. Instead they are hunting from the start, foraging on the flanks. They hope to flush and spear wallabies, lizards, emus or bandicoots. From time to time they fire an area of brush and then go over the smoking stubble to pick up roasted lizards and baked bilbies. If bilbies remain hiding underground, women use their all-purpose platters to fan smoke into burrows and drive them up for air.

"The older men lead the procession and some of them wing out from the rear of it to assess the prowess of the hunters ahead and to watch over the women and children straggling along in the rear guard. Women teach children how to dig out sweet fatty witjuti grubs from *Acacia* roots, how to spot subterranean homes of bloated honey ants, how to reap seeding grass.

"Lunchtime: we come to small hill of granite near foot of which lies inconspicuous boulder. Leader lifts off boulder, ladles out handful of water from narrow-necked, urn-sized catchment underneath. We all take our turns, then lounge about resting. One grandmother, complaining all the while that women's work is never done, rests her hands against a tree and seems to be rubbing out a cigarette butt in cranny under her feet. I see that in the cranny are grass grains she has collected and is now threshing. When husks are off, she separates seeds from dirt by rocking them in her wooden dish.

B y midafternoon we reach our water hole. The ground around it is covered with kurrajong seeds, left by birds which eat kurrajong fruit pods. There must be at least a bushel. Women look impressed, get to work first cleaning seeds, shaking out dirt in dishes, then roasting seeds, shaking them some more with live coals from fire. They shake out embers, grind seeds with flat stones, mix flour with water, put final product into fire as patties for baking. Later in afternoon men bring in one rock wallaby, one spiny anteater. Shallow pits are excavated with digging sticks and scooping plates, game put into them and covered with coals and hot ashes. Anteater first wetted down so that its skin will steam loose. Wallaby dug up several times so that tasty juices can be drained from it through incisions in groin. Cook pits might turn out palatable clambake by midnight but everyone too hungry to wait. Half-cooked meat is exhumed too soon and bones are gnawed clean. All members of party share in food according to established custom. Here, hunter's uncle gets a choice leg while aged aunt gets a bit of belly skin. In other tribes division of spoils would be different. In some, hunter himself would receive nothing.

"After dinner women collect kindling and light sleeping fires. Men assist in building windbreaks, repair old spears and make new ones. They straighten out bends by heating in the fire, grease them with fat to prevent splitting, replace sinew lashings which have worn thin. Children let off steam in the quiet, well-behaved way typical of many primitive societies. Finally, everyone coats himself in grease and ashes as if to swim the Channel, and nestles in between sleeping fires, infants in mothers' arms. The fitful night begins and adults everywhere are getting up at intervals to tend those miserable little fires."

Not every day in the life of an aboriginal is as easy or as hard as the one just described. There are times on the desert when a family group can camp by one water hole for days on end before food begins to grow scarce; there are times, too, when the morning dew must be mopped from the leaves with

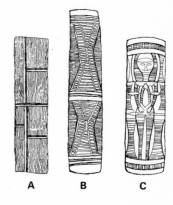

A   B   C

Message sticks, small carved wooden tablets, are used by many tribes as reminders of debts, as passports to guarantee the safety of a messenger in hostile territory and as invitations to ceremonies, hunts and battles.

Stick A (above) is a shopping list, noting on one side the goods wanted by a woman and on the other those needed by her husband. Stick B is an I.O.U., reminding the debtor, to whom it will be delivered, that he owes 16 different items, including hair oil, fishhooks, two undershirts and a comb. The four crescent shapes indicate how many moons the debt has gone unpaid. Stick C is a ceremonial message. It represents the funeral of a mythical figure, Buma-Buma, and is sent to a group of people who have a boy ready to be circumcised.

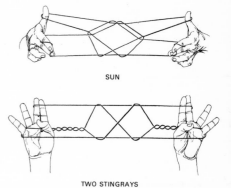

SUN

TWO STINGRAYS

Aborigines manipulate bark-fiber string into over 400 distinct cat's-cradle designs, for amusement and to tell one another stories. Making string figures is primarily a woman's pastime but the men make certain figures for use in their rituals. The figures for Sun and Two Stingrays with Young are literal representations, but many figures are abstract, bearing no resemblance to their subjects.

A HOUSE FOR ALL SEASONS

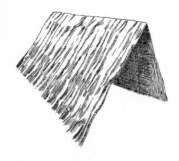

Since most aborigines are nomadic for part of every year, they have no need for permanent homes. Instead, they make temporary houses to suit the weather. During the cold, dry winters, some build tentlike shelters with large sheets of bark.

In the heart of the wet season, the natives of Arnhem Land construct beehive huts by thatching a bark-sided igloo with grasses. At night, the family retreats inside, plugs the doorway with grass and lights a fire to smoke the insects out.

During the months of scattered showers, when mosquitoes are still a menace, the men erect sleeping platforms, elevating them on stilts four to six feet from the ground so that smoky fires may be lit under them. They are then roofed with bark.

sponges of fine grass; times when every available root, stem and buried frog is milked of its teacupful of liquid; times when the nearest water seems too far to walk to and a clan will gamble instead on a crack where a kangaroo was seen to sniff or an ant to emerge fat with juice. Then the crack is laboriously widened and a new water hole opened up. On successive visits over the years, the clan may widen and deepen this fissure until it has become a well, descending through as much as 15 feet of stones, sand or river bed.

The aborigines of the damp coastal regions seldom feel the awe of drought as do the plains nomads, but they have their own hardships and their own subtle stratagems to practice on nature. Two separate beach tribes, one in the east and one in the south, practice "magic" to make friends with the dolphins offshore and teach them, by dint of fishy kickbacks, to work as submarine sheep dogs, herding fish into nets.

Knowing the seasons—the times of winds, heat and cold, the times at which a bird would be nesting in this district or a plant fruiting in that—requires a working mental calendar. Many tides and turnings of nature are duly noted by all tribes—in some, by the rising of the Pleiades in May.

For some coastal aborigines, the time of greatest dearth is the rainy season. Groups such as the Arnhem Landers anticipate it by building bark-roofed shelters in which they wait out the torrential wet, huddling around small, smoky fires, slapping at mosquitoes and sand flies and painting handsome designs on their hut ceilings. After the mire and misery, when the wallabies were once more hopping, the megapodes mounding, the fish spawning and the turtles trundling on the beaches, the coast dwellers would indulge their stomachs just as gluttonously as would their desert brethren after a successful hunt in the red center. The reputation that some of them later earned as prodigious eaters was often the result of showing off before white men; in ordinary times, the tribes usually got enough to eat and felt no compulsion to stuff themselves.

On the beach or in the desert, a time of plenty calls for a native festival, or "corroboree." Some corroborees are small affairs at which kinsmen gather to stamp out story dances, intone epic chants and keep time by droning down wooden tubes called didgeridoos. Usually the proceedings are lit by the flicker of many small grass bonfires. In parts of the south they used to be illuminated by the spectacular torch of a blazing hollow tree trunk. Other bigger corroborees involve all the clans from hundreds of miles around, and at these, pleasure is usually leavened with solemn business between the gathered elders of the tribe. Religious mysteries and initiations are performed for days on end. Rituals are discussed tirelessly. Marriages are arranged years ahead.

THE taboos and totems, rituals and deities in which the aborigines believe have evolved slowly in their minds for thousands of years and have become endlessly elaborate. Magic invades every aspect of aboriginal life. It is used in medicine, rain making, hunting, fishing, love making, sorcery, in the increase of plants and animals and the ensuring of food supplies. It is also employed to uphold laws and customs. A tribesman lives in constant intimate association with a complex of "religious mysteries" which involve detailed knowledge about rites, beliefs, spirits, sacred places, paths, objects, ceremonies, dances, legends —even the spiritual aspects of arts and crafts. Every mature aboriginal, in short, must carry in his head a quantity of information rivaling that of a college professor, and most of it connected with magic and ritual.

When an Australian aboriginal adapts himself to the steel age, not one, but two gulfs are crossed: the first from Old and Middle Stone Age food collecting to New Stone Age husbandry; the second from there on out into the individualism and science of the modern world. Of the two, the first probably yawns the wider. How much wider can be appreciated by considering the New Stone Age Maori of New Zealand. These enterprising voyagers are believed to have reached their islands a scant thousand years ago. At first they probably arrived as castaways in outriggers driven far off course by storms. Later, perhaps, they came in an organized fleet directed by some helmsman who had made the return journey from New Zealand to his balmy home islands in east central Polynesia. Archeology supports the idea of a few stray canoes. Maori tradition supports the idea of a single "Great Fleet."

However they came, the Maori evidently landed close to starvation because none of their domestic animals survived the voyage except dogs. Of their plants, the breadfruits, bananas and coconuts probably died in the cold winter, leaving them nothing but taro and sweet potatoes. With only these two carryovers from their previous culture, they improvised a livelihood out of what they found. For want of the bark of the paper mulberry tree in which to clothe themselves, they discovered New Zealand flax and learned how to process and weave it. For lack of the materials to make sewn-plank outriggers, they taught .themselves to hew dugouts from the great native kauri pines. For lack of pigs and poultry, they possibly hunted and finally exterminated the giant moas.

T HE flexibility with which the Maori adapted to their new temperate environment was only matched by the good sense they showed, centuries later, in being hostile and suspicious toward the first white men. When Abel Janzoon Tasman discovered the green New Zealand coast in 1642, he promptly started ashore and just as promptly lost a few members of his crew to an unfriendly reception committee. When Captain James Cook rediscovered the islands 127 years later, he was rebuffed in all attempts to explore the interior. In the decades that followed, however, the adaptiveness of the Maori proved their undoing. Quick to appreciate the virtues of English blankets and firearms, they gradually permitted whalers, traders and missionaries to establish posts along their shores. A Maori chief took a trip to England and returned with the idea of unifying the tribes under his own enlightened Western-style monarchy. Armsrunners supplied both him and the chiefs who opposed him with guns. Soon his dream had foundered in a sea of blood, and Europeans were gradually buying up the tribal lands of the vanquished.

By mid-19th Century, enough of New Zealand was in the hands of the outlanders to make the Maori join forces to resist further encroachment. In the famous Maori wars from 1860 to 1870, they matched reckless courage and ferocity against the superior discipline and fire power of British regulars and colonial militia. When peace was finally signed, less than 50,000 Maori remained out of an original population of perhaps 100,000. Although the survivors were given special representation in the New Zealand parliament, they were crowded onto unwanted lands amounting to about one sixteenth of their original holdings. There they at first languished, and by 1900 only 40,000 of them were left. But since then, largely through the efforts of their own chiefs, they have staged an astounding resurgence. Over 100,000 strong, they now maintain themselves as a proud minority, economically self-sufficient and culturally distinct within the New Zealand nation.

The history of the Maori breathes with the spirit of the New Stone Age, a spirit which, in a mere 6,000 years, has catapulted man on through later barriers of stone, bronze, iron and steel into the atomic era. Suddenly a great flexibility, opportunism and inventiveness have arisen in the ranks of mankind. Sensing its tumult, the hidebound Paleolithic aborigines of Australia seem to stand demoralized. They give up and disappear with hardly more protest, hardly more understanding of their own tragedy than the mute marsupials around them.

In the great living laboratory of Australia, scientists have learned that the process of extinction is not entirely mysterious but can be explained, in part, by the rigid dependence of an animal, human or otherwise, on his food-gathering territory. In 1958 the zoologist B. J. Marlow published a most revealing survey of the damage that settlement has done to the marsupials of New South Wales. This is one of the smallest and most thickly settled states in Australia. That is to say, it has about the same area as Texas and Louisiana combined and only 31 per cent of the population. Marlow discovered that of 52 species of New South Wales marsupials, 11 have not been seen since 1910 and can be presumed extinct. More important, he found that the extent of extinction depends on the amount of transformation wrought in animal habitats by herding and planting. None of the rain forest species were extinct, only 8 per cent of the *Eucalyptus* forest species, only 12 to 9 per cent of the species in broken woodland, but a monstrous 42.8 per cent of the species normally inhabiting open country.

THE lesson is clear: like the aborigines, wild animals live or die with their hunting grounds. If modern men go on doubling their numbers every century as they have in the last, few animal habitats will long remain intact, even in empty Australia, except for the little world of shrubs at the bottom of each garden. At this prospect poets wince, philosophers despair and men of affairs understandably shrug their shoulders. The idealist sees *Homo sapiens* reducing the more than a million other products of three billion years on earth to pockets and parks—to tiny unbalanced, evolutionarily sterile populations. The pragmatist sees extinction as a natural process and knows man for an unreformed natural creature—a species which will compete, and exercise its overwhelming superiority, come what may.

What mere human beings can do against their own proclivities is obviously an immensely complicated problem in terms of specific legislation and international agreements. The two broad paths any solution must take, however, are so obvious that it hardly seems possible that individuals and entire institutions refuse to recognize them. In the next few decades human beings must find a way to stop multiplying and they must set aside large tracts of wild land—not mere recreation areas but extensive wildernesses where plants and animals can maintain some measure of normal ecological balance.

If this is not done, the self-proclaimed master of creation, who is just beginning to understand the chemistry of life, may some day find himself working in a sterile laboratory and dying for want of some contaminant, some trace ingredient. It is not that all men are likely to catch some new kind of cold and perish for want of an extinct mold which might have supplied an antibiotic. It is rather that we must nurse all the possibilities if our searching civilization is to go on realizing itself. What a pity it would be if a young biochemist, two or three centuries from now—a man equipped to understand and make use of the genetic combinations in various forms of living cells—should yearn for a platypus egg and not be able to obtain it, or for a phalanger foetus and know that the last had died decades before he himself was born.

FOUR TRIBESMEN, BODIES WHITENED WITH CLAY, JOIN IN A DANCE THAT IMITATES THE COURTSHIP MOVEMENTS OF THE BROLGA CRANE

The Aboriginal Australians

Australia's aborigines are the sole survivors of a distinct human race, the Australoid, of which about 41,000 full bloods remain from a population that was nearly 300,000 at the time of white settlement only 175 years ago. In 25,000 years, they have developed few tools other than simple spears, boomerangs and flint knives, but they possess a complex social and ceremonial system.

A MILLINGIMBI WOMAN, whose tribe inhabits the rich area between the Arafura Sea and inland forests, digs for roots while her children forage for bark insects, nuts and lizards.

The Ties That Bind

The aboriginal is a food gatherer and hunter. He has never planted a crop, trained an animal, bred a bird. He has settled—like the animals—in groups no larger than the land can support. But because no area can supply all the needs of even a single family, the aborigines have developed social ties with other groups in a complex system of mutual interdependence.

A man's first kinship is to his family, consisting of his wife, or wives, and children. He belongs to a clan, two or more closely related families who own land and take a ritual name. His clan and others may form a horde, a food-gathering unit which controls all the water and wildlife in the combined territory but has no ritual identity. The final unit is the tribe, which may link men living hundreds of miles apart and who rarely see one another, but who share a language and culture. Tribes contain from 250 to 700 individuals, usually have no common ancestor or mythology and no central leader.

A GOULBURN ISLANDER aims with an iron-tipped fish spear while his companions steady the dugout canoe. Coastal tribes have a better diet and travel less than those from the interior.

A DESERT FAMILY camps on a rocky slope after a hard day's "walk-about" during which the men hunted for kangaroos while the women and children scoured the ground for snails, bird's eggs and edible plants. Because the food supply in arid Central Australia is so limited, desert dwellers must travel almost daily. Tribal lands may encompass 40,000 square miles.

A BARK PAINTING from Arnhem Land shows two kangaroos, a marsupial rat, a goanna, an emu, a long-necked turtle, and a straw bag with yams and roots sticking out. The paint-ing was done on the prepared inside surface of the bark of a *Eucalyptus* tree. Paints consist of red and yellow ochre, pipe clay, and charcoal mixed with water and the juice of orchids.

CARVED WOODEN FIGURES, carefully painted, are stacked up prior to being used in the "Dance of the Flying Fox," which tells the tale of two red flying fox brothers who murder other flying foxes and are finally carried off into the sky by a black flying fox. Like many aboriginal dances and legends, this one has a moral: members of a clan should never kill each other.

Art for Man's Sake

Artistic expression of many kinds plays an important part in the life of aborigines. They paint on bark, carve wood, engrave rocks, decorate tools and adorn their own bodies. Much of this art serves a ritual function. The hunter, for example, who cannot always be sure of finding game, may chant a ritual song while painting an animal-filled scene, such as that shown at left, to ensure success on his next hunt. He thus fulfills his ritual duty so that nature will fulfill hers, which is to produce food. He believes that if he fails, nature will also fail. However, the hunter may omit the sacred chant and paint the same scene simply to amuse himself. In either case, the painting itself seldom has any value or significance to him and he is likely to discard it when finished. It is the act of doing the painting, of giving his own energy, which is important to him.

SPITTING PAINT from his mouth, an Oënpelli tribesman decorates a friend with a clan pattern. Body painting serves as spiritual "make-up," turning the wearer into a ritual hero.

A STRAW BAG is filled with ripe fruits from a cycad palm. Although poisonous, soaking and peeling will make them edible.

TWO PLAYFUL GIRLS toy with a mangrove crab. When these girls marry, they will move into their husbands' territory and

A DEAD WALLABY lies beside the spear and woomera that killed it. Skinned and dressed, it may yield 30 pounds of meat.

Food Is Everybody's Business

Having no domesticated animals and knowing no agriculture, the aboriginal must spend most of his time looking for food, and his activities vary greatly with the seasons. Each part of the continent has its own cycle of ripening, of plenty and want, and the rhythm of native life is carefully attuned to it. For example, the people of Blue Mud Bay in Arnhem Land engage in six different seasonal activities. In April, they are emerging from a two-month wet spell, living in big camps on high ground and beginning to organize goose and fish hunting expeditions. As the land dries, they break camp and start

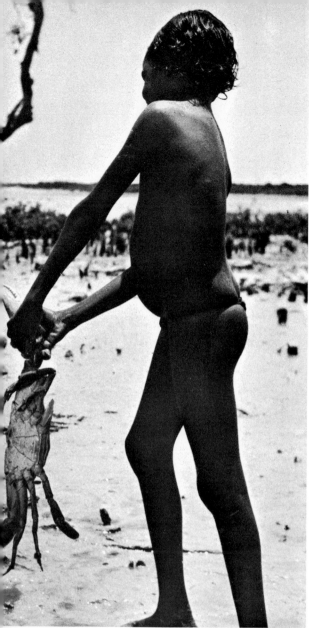

have to face all over again the task of learning a region's food supply. Boys work with the women until they are initiated.

TWO GOANNAS that have been flushed from the scrub by dingoes and caught by hand are carried home by a hunter.

wandering, burning large grass tracts to make travel easier. At the height of the hot dry season, travel slows down, the fruits of the cycad palm form the staple diet, and much ceremonial activity takes place. In late October, the "nose of the wet season," the people congregate once more, and two months later, with the actual breaking of the rains, they mark the end of the palm-fruit harvest and settle into wet-season camps. Then torrential rains and flooding restrict the natives to an almost sedentary life; they live on dried fruits and nuts and whatever small game the men are able to capture.

A STING RAY'S POISON BARB, which may be used as a spear tip, is cut off by a fisherman who holds the tail in his teeth.

MIMICKING A KANGAROO, A GOULBURN ISLANDER HOPS INTO THE AIR WHILE AN ELDER PRETENDS TO LAUNCH A SPEAR. THE MEN ARE PA

A Dance for Every Occasion

Aborigines dance at the slightest excuse. Secular dances are done at funerals, weddings, to celebrate trades and simply to express happiness. The steps are usually simple—a skip, a shuffle, a syncopated stomp—but exuberant.

Sacred dances are much more serious. They act

TOTEMIC PATTERNS, ALTHOUGH THIS DANCE, PART OF A CORROBOREE, IS IN FUN. A RITUAL VERSION EXISTS FOR MORE SOLEMN OCCASIONS

out myths, aim to increase food species, and mark the time when boys become men. Dance music is provided by the clapping of boomerangs, the drone of the didjeridoo flute and the singing of onlookers. Ritual dances follow prescribed steps whose patterns are known only by the initiated. But there is room for innovation and certain men become noted for their excellence, although there are no professionals. Women do not participate in the main dance but stand apart doing subdued steps of their own. Boys often dance in secular performances but are barred from adult ceremonies until initiation.

The Ordeals of Manhood

The aboriginal male must undergo a variety of unusual trials before he is fully accepted as an adult. These "rites of passage" gradually introduce to him the secret myths and legends of the tribe, known only to initiated men. Up to the age of six or eight, a boy works with the women and has no status. Then he is "stolen" from them for the first in a series of initiation ceremonies, which may include circumcision, the knocking out of a front tooth, the incising of chest and arm scars, and the plucking of hair from his face and body. A boy suffers these "ritual deaths" to be reborn a man. At later celebrations, and when he witnesses the initiation of others, he learns more tribal ways. Girls are not initiated but must learn certain duties, customs, and legends which are revealed only to women.

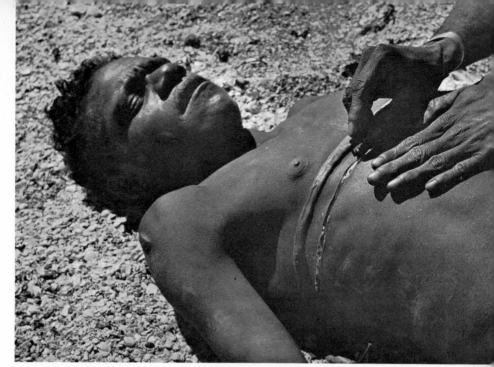

AN ABORIGINAL YOUTH grimaces manfully while a fresh decorative scar is cut into his chest. Ashes will be rubbed in the wound to fester it and to cause a larger mark. Scars may signify initiation stages or be simply to beautify the wearer.

WRITHING IN THE ARMS of their sponsors, two eight-year-old boys undergo circumcision. The operation, once done with a stone knife, is now done with a razor blade. Hot ashes are used to close the wound.

A TRIBAL INITIATE kneels quietly while blood from his teacher's arm flows down his back. Sacred blood baths give the youth strength to bear the sight of secrets and symbols which will be revealed to him.

LADEN WITH PROVISIONS bought with money he earned from selling crocodile skins, a tribal elder returns from the mission store. Missionaries encourage such trading to teach natives how to use money.

A Dark Past, a Muddy Future

When Britain lost America as a penal colony, she turned to Australia and, in 1788, established the first permanent white settlement of prisoners at Sydney. As convicts were released and free men came to colonize, they pushed into the fertile areas, killing and uprooting the aborigines as they went. Murdered by white men's guns, infected by their diseases, driven from homesites as the land was put to agriculture, the natives died in great numbers. In 1921, when the first official census was taken, the aboriginal population had been cut by 75 per cent. As late as 1928, white officials who had killed 32 natives in reprisal for a suspected crime were acquitted in court. Although the slaughter has stopped, the number of full-blooded aborigines has until recently declined every year. While it is true that the number of mixed bloods is on the rise, the dying out of the tribalized natives and their ways is a profound loss both to Australian culture and to the world.

LEARNING TO READ, two girls study primers at a mission school. There were about 500 native languages, but they are being forgotten as English is taught. Schooling of almost all aborigines stops at 14.

Bibliography

Geography and Geology

Audas, James Wales, *The Australian Bushland*. W. A. Hamer Proprietary, Ltd., North Melbourne, 1950.

Commonwealth Scientific and Industrial Research Organization, Australia, in association with Melbourne University Press, *The Australian Environment* (3rd ed.). Cambridge University Press, 1960.

David, Sir T. W. Edgeworth, *The Geology of the Commonwealth of Australia*. Edward Arnold & Co., 1950.

Finlayson, H. H., *The Red Centre*. Angus & Robertson, Ltd., London, 1952.

Gilluly, James, A. C. Waters and A. O. Woodford, *Principles of Geology*. W. H. Freeman & Co., 1959.

Keast, Allen, *Window to Bushland*. The Educational Press, Sydney, 1959.

Osborn, Fairfield, ed., *The Pacific World*. W. W. Norton & Co., 1944.

Skemp, J. R., *Tasmania*. Macmillan, 1958.

Smith, Bernard, *European Vision and the South Pacific*. Clarendon Press, 1960.

Stamp, L. Dudley, *A Regional Geography* (Part III), *Australia and New Zealand* (7th ed.). John Wiley & Sons, 1961.

Taylor, Griffith, *Australia*. E. P. Dutton & Co., 1943.

Wallace, Alfred Russel, *The Malay Archipelago*. Dover, 1962.

Plants

Forestry and Timber Bureau, Department of the Interior, Commonwealth of Australia, *Forest Trees of Australia*. 1957.

Gardner, C. A., *Wildflowers of Western Australia*. Western Australian Newspapers, Ltd., Perth, 1959.

Harris, Thistle Y., *Wild Flowers of Australia* (5th ed.). Angus & Robertson, Ltd., Sydney, 1962.

Jacobs, M. R., *Growth Habits of the Eucalypts*. Forestry and Timber Bureau, Canberra, 1955.

Martin, W., *The New Zealand Nature Book*, *The Flora of New Zealand* (Vol. II). Whitcombe & Tombs, Ltd., 1929.

McLuckie, John, and H. S. McKee, *Australian and New Zealand Botany*. Associated General Publications, Sydney, 1954.

Seward, A. C., *Plant Life Through the Ages* (2nd ed.). Hafner, 1959.

Invertebrates

Curran, C. H., *Insects of the Pacific World* (2nd ed.). Macmillan, 1945.

Klots, Alexander B. and Elsie B., *Living Insects of the World*. Doubleday, 1959.

McKeown, Keith C., *Australian Spiders* (2nd ed.). Angus & Robertson, Ltd., Sydney, 1952. *Insect Wonders of Australia*. Angus & Robertson, Ltd., Sydney, 1935.

Tillyard, R. J., *The Insects of Australia and New Zealand*. Angus & Robertson, Ltd., Sydney, 1926.

Fishes, Amphibians and Reptiles

Cochran, Doris M., *Living Amphibians of the World*. Doubleday, 1961.

Herald, Earl S., *Living Fishes of the World*. Doubleday, 1961.

Kinghorn, J. R., *The Snakes of Australia* (2nd ed.). Michigan State University Press, 1957.

Loveridge, Arthur, *Reptiles of the Pacific World* (2nd ed.). Macmillan, 1945.

Parker, H. W., *Snakes*. W. W. Norton & Company, Inc., 1963.

Phillips, W. J., *Nature in New Zealand: Native Fishes* (rev. ed.). A. H. & A. W. Reed, Wellington, 1953.

Rooij, Nelly de, *The Reptiles of the Indo-Australian Archipelago*. E. J. Brill, 1915.

Schmidt, Karl P., and Robert F. Inger, *Living Reptiles of the World*. Doubleday, 1957.

Waite, Edgar R. (H. M. Hale, ed.), *The Reptiles and Amphibians of South Australia*. Government Printers, Adelaide, 1929.

Mammals

Burrell, Harry, *The Platypus*. Angus & Robertson, Ltd., Sydney, 1927.

Fleay, David, *We Breed the Platypus*. Robertson & Mullens, Melbourne, 1944.

Harper, Francis, *Extinct and Vanishing Mammals of the Old World*. American Committee for International Wild Life Protection, 1945.

Laurie, Eleanor M. O., and J. E. Hill, *List of Land Mammals of New Guinea, Celebes and Adjacent Islands, 1758-1952*. British Museum of Natural History, 1954.

Jones, Frederic Wood, *The Mammals of South Australia* (3 vols.). R. E. E. Rogers, Government Printers, Adelaide, 1923-1925.

Troughton, Ellis, *Furred Animals of Australia* (6th ed.). Angus & Robertson, Ltd., Sydney, 1955.

Birds

Cayley, Neville W., *What Bird Is That?* Angus & Robertson, Ltd., Sydney, 1959.

Chisholm, Alexander H., *Bird Wonders of Australia*. Michigan State University Press, 1958. *The Romance of the Lyrebird*. Angus & Robertson, Ltd., Sydney, 1960.

Frith, H. J., *The Mallee-fowl*. Angus & Robertson, Ltd., Sydney, 1962.

Gilliard, E. Thomas, *Living Birds of the World*. Doubleday, 1958.

Greenway, James C., Jr., *Extinct and Vanishing Birds of the World*. American Committee for International Wild Life Protection, New York, 1958.

Iredale, Tom, *Birds of New Guinea* (Vols. I and II). Georgian House, Melbourne, 1956.

Leach, J. A., *An Australian Bird Book*. Whitcombe & Tombs, Ltd., 1961.

Marshall, Alexander J., *Bower Birds*. Oxford University Press, 1954.

Mayr, Ernst, *Birds of the Southwest Pacific*. Macmillan, 1947.

Oliver, W. R. B., *New Zealand Birds*. A. H. & A. W. Reed, Wellington, 1955.

Serventy, D. L., and H. M. Whittell, *A Handbook of the Birds of Western Australia*. Patersons Press, Ltd., Perth, 1948.

Soper, M. F., *New Zealand Bird Portraits*. Whitcombe & Tombs, Ltd., 1963.

Williams, Gordon R., *Birds of New Zealand*. A. H. & A. W. Reed, Wellington, 1963.

Man

Coon, Carleton S., *The Origin of Races*. Alfred A. Knopf, 1962. *The Story of Man*. Alfred A. Knopf, 1962.

Elkin, A. P., *The Australian Aborigines*. Angus & Robertson, Ltd., Sydney, 1938.

Elkin, A. P., and Catherine and Ronald Berndt, *Art in Arnhem Land*. F. W. Chesire, Ltd., Melbourne, 1950.

Mander, Linden A., *Some Dependent Peoples of the South Pacific*. Macmillan, 1954.

Meggit, M. J., *Desert People*. Angus & Robertson, Ltd., Sydney, 1962.

Mountford, C. P., *Brown Men and Red Sand: Wanderings in Wild Australia*. Phoenix House, Ltd., 1951.

Oliver, Douglas L., *The Pacific Islands*. Doubleday Anchor Books, American Museum of Nat. Hist., 1961.

Tindale, Norman B., and H. A. Lindsay, *Aboriginal Australians*. Jacaranda Press, 1963.

Warner, W. Lloyd, *A Black Civilization*. Harper and Brothers, 1958.

Miscellaneous

Barrett, Charles, *Wild Life of Australia and New Guinea*. William Heinemann, Ltd., 1954.

Darlington, Phillip J., Jr., *Zoogeography: The Geographical Distribution of Animals*. John Wiley & Sons, 1957.

Keast, A., R. L. Crocker and C. S. Christian, eds., *Biogeography and Ecology in Australia*. Uitgeverig Dr. W. Junk, 1959.

Le Souef, A. S., and Harry Burrell, *The Wild Animals of Australasia*. George G. Harrap, 1926.

Mountford, Charles P., *Records of the American Australian Scientific Expedition to Arnhem Land* (Vols. I and II). Melbourne University Press, Melbourne, 1956.

Powell, A. W. B., *Native Animals of New Zealand*. The Unity Press, Ltd., 1961.

Field Guides

Common, I. F. B., *Australian Moths*. Jacaranda Press.

Goadby, Peter, *Sharks & Predatory Fish*. Jacaranda Press.

Keast, Allen, *Some Bush Birds of Australia*. Jacaranda Press.

Marlow, Basil, *Marsupials of Australia*. Jacaranda Press.

McMichael, Donald, *Shells of the Seashore*. Jacaranda Press.

McPhee, D. R., *Snakes and Lizards of Australia*. Jacaranda Press.

Oakman, H., *Some Trees of Australia*. Jacaranda Press.

Riek, Edgar, *Insects of Australia*. Jacaranda Press.

Whitley, Gilbert, *Marine Fishes* (2 vols.). Jacaranda Press. *Native Freshwater Fishes*. Jacaranda Press.

Like many of the books on this page, these guides may be available only through British or Australian publishers.

193

Credits

The sources for the illustrations in this book are shown below. Credits for pictures from left to right are separated by commas, top to bottom by dashes.

Cover—Graham Pizzey
8—George Leavens
12, 13—Drawings by Otto van Eersel
17—Frank Hurley
18, 19—Maps by Matt Greene
20, 21—Eric Lindgren—J.N. Jennings
22, 23—Howard Hughes
24, 25—Raymond N. Davie, Gordon DeLisle—Frank Hurley from Rapho-Guillumette, Fritz Goro
26—Robin Smith
27—A. B. Costain—Janet E. R. Finch
28, 29—Dr. Frits Went, Neville Moderate—Ederic Slater
30—Brian Brake from Magnum —Robin Smith
31—George Silk
32—Douglass Baglin
34, 35—Drawings by Otto van Eersel from *Australia* by Griffith Taylor, E.P. Dutton & Co. Inc. and Methuen & Co. Ltd. London
39—Drawing by Anthony Saris
40, 41—Drawings by René Martin
42—Drawings by John Newcomb
43—Queensland Government
44—Axel Poignant except top right George Leavens
45—Axel Poignant, Allen Keast —Fritz Goro, Vincent Serventy
46, 47—Forestry Commission of New South Wales, G. Chippendale
48—Douglass Baglin
49—Frank Hurley—Hal Missingham, Douglass Baglin
50—Norman Chaffer
51—B. J. Gorey—Vincent Serventy, Kay Breeden
52—Norman Chaffer, Rod Warnock—C. A. Gardner (2)—Kay Breeden—G. W. Althofer
53—Anthony Healy, Vincent Serventy—Eric Lindgren, John S.

Clark, R. Gibbons, W. H. Butler—C. A. Gardner, Michael K. Morcombe
54, 55—left Robin Smith—F. G. McKenzie right; L. Friar—H. Fairlie-Cuninghame, Alan Hewer—J. S. Womersley, H. Fairlie-Cuninghame—Ederic Slater
56, 57—left Norman Chaffer—Ederic Slater center; K. G. Roberts except bottom right; Anthony Healy right; Allen Keast, Anthony Healy—Kay Breeden
58—W. R. Gasking
62, 63—Drawings by Stephen Chan
64, 65—Drawings by Margaret E. Estey
67—Drawing by Margaret E. Estey
68, 69—W. R. Gasking; drawings by Rudolf Freund
70—John Dominis
71—David Fleay
72, 73—Drawings by Margaret E. Estey
74, 75—Sven Gillsater, John Dominis except top F. J. Mitchell
76—Eric Lindgren
79—Drawing by Chett Rennesson
80—Drawings by Rudolf Freund
81—Drawing by Guy Tudor
82, 83—Drawings by Stephen Rogers Peck
85—David Fleay
86, 87—Drawings by Jean Zallinger; reconstruction by William G. Huff
88, 89—Drawings by Jean Zallinger; background by Otto van Eersel
90—B. J. G. Marlow
91—E. Rotherham—B. P. Bertram
92, 93—David Fleay—Eric Lindgren, Allen Keast
94—Don Stephens—David Fleay

95—Graham Pizzey
96—Australian National Travel Association
98, 99—Drawings by Rudolf Freund
100—Drawings by Rudolf Freund
103—Drawings by Guy Tudor
107—David Fleay
108—John Dominis, Kay Breeden
109—David Fleay, Anne Ulrich
110—Michael K. Morcombe
111—Ina Watson, John Dominis
112—George Leavens—George Leavens from Photo Researchers, Inc.
113—George Leavens—Allen Keast
114, 115—Eric Worrell, David Fleay
116, 117—George Leavens
118—I. D. Hiscock—Janet E. R. Finch, Eric Worrell—Peter Slater, John Warham
119—David Moore, David Fleay —W. N. Holsworth, John Dominis—Eric Howell, H. B. Shugg
120, 121—John Dominis
122, 123—Ederic Slater CSIRO
124, 125—Ralph Morse; Kangaroo Victoria courtesy Animal Talent Scouts, New York City
126—David Fleay
131—Drawing by Mark Binn
132, 133—Drawings by Frances Zweifel
134, 135—Drawings by René Martin
137—I. F. B. Common
138, 139—Vincent Serventy— Ederic Slater
140—Peter Slater
141—Betty Hadlington—Allen Keast
142, 143—Kay Breeden—Harold C. Cogger (2), Eric Lindgren, Ray D. Mackay
144—top David Fleay; bottom J. Carter

145—K. G. Roberts
146—Michael K. Morcombe
148, 149—Drawings by Guy Tudor
151, 152—Drawings by Guy Tudor
155—Ina Watson
156, 157—Janet E. R. Finch— Alwyn Y. Pepper, Harold J. Pollock, Norman Chaffer, Harold J. Pollock from Free Lance Photographers Guild
158—John Anderson
159—Robin Smith except top l National Photo Library, New Zealand
160, 161—Ederic Slater, Neville Moderate
162—John Dominis
163—Axel Poignant—Dr. M. F Soper
164—top H. J. Frith, Roy P. Cooper; bottom L. H. Smith
165—H. J. Frith—L. H. Smith
166—Eric Lindgren—John Warham
167—Sven Gillsater
168—Axel Poignant
172—Drawings by Anthony Saris
173—Drawings by Anthony Saris courtesy the Australian Museum, Sydney
174, 175—Drawings by Anthony Saris
176—Drawings by Otto van Ee
179—Harold J. Pollock
180—Fritz Goro
181—K. Meyers
182—Fritz Goro
183—Fritz Goro—Frederick D McCarthy
184, 185—Fritz Goro except center Axel Poignant
186, 187—Fritz Goro
188, 189—Fritz Goro except bottom right Jens Bjerre
190, 191—Fritz Goro
Back Cover—Otto van Eersel

Acknowledgments

The editors of this book are particularly indebted to Allen Keast, Department of Biology, Queen's University, Kingston, Ontario, who read the book in its entirety. They are also indebted to François Bourlière, Professor, Faculté de Médecine de Paris; Leonard J. Brass, Associate Curator, Archbold Collections, Department of Mammalogy, The American Museum of Natural History; William Bridges, Curator of Publications, New York Zoological Society; Nancy Burbridge, Australian National Herbarium, Canberra; Mr. and Mrs. Bern D'Essen; Robert L. Edwards, Assistant Director, Biological Laboratory, U.S. Bureau of Commercial Fisheries, Woods Hole; David Fleay, Director of Fauna Reserve, West Burleigh, Queensland; H. J. Frith, Chief, Division of Wildlife Research, Commonwealth Scientific Industrial Research Organization, Canberra; O. P. Gabites, Consul General of New Zealand, New York; Margaret Gail, Librarian, Australian National Library; Willis J. Gertsch, Curator, Department of Entomology, The American Museum of Natural History; E. Thomas Gilliard, Associate Curator, Department of Ornithology, The American Museum of Natural History; Fritz Goro, LIFE Staff Photographer; Milton Hildebrand, Professor of Zoology, University of California; Sidney Horenstein, Scientific Assistant, Department of Fossil Invertebrates, The American Museum of

Natural History; F. B. Hubbard; Richard M. Klein, Curator of Plar Physiology, New York Botanical Garden; George Leavens; F. D. Mc Carthy, Curator of Anthropology, The Australian Museum, Sydne John A. Moore, Professor of Zoology, Columbia University; Davi Potts; R. A. Stirton, Professor of Paleontology, Curator of Mamma and Director of the Museum of Paleontology, University of California Ray Strong, Artist in Residence, Santa Barbara Museum of Natur History; Richard H. Tedford, Assistant Professor of Geology, Universit of California; Norman B. Tindale, Assistant Director, South Australia Museum, Adelaide; Hobart M. Van Deusen, Assistant Curator, Arch bold Collections, Department of Mammalogy, The American Museur of Natural History; Richard G. Van Gelder, Chairman and Associat Curator, Department of Mammalogy, The American Museum of Natu ral History; Andrew P. Vayda, Assistant Professor of Anthropolog Columbia University; Carl L. Withner, Associate Professor of Biology Brooklyn College; Michael O. Woodburn, University of California Richard G. Zweifel, Associate Curator, Department of Herpetolog The American Museum of Natural History; The Australian Referenc Library at the Australian Consulate-General, New York; and the L brary of The American Museum of Natural History.

Index

Numerals in italics indicate a photograph or painting of the subject mentioned.

PRODUCTION STAFF FOR TIME INCORPORATED
Arthur R. Murphy Jr. (*Vice President and Director of Production*), Robert E. Foy, James P. Menton and Caroline Ferri
Text photocomposed under the direction of Albert J. Dunn and Arthur J. Dunn

x

Printed by R. R. Donnelley & Sons Company, Crawfordsville, Indiana,
and Livermore and Knight Co., a division of Printing Corporation of America, Providence, Rhode Island
Bound by R. R. Donnelley & Sons Company, Crawfordsville, Indiana
Paper by The Mead Corporation, Dayton, Ohio